AF486716

A Bronx Memoir of Justice and Belonging

Darney "K Born" Rivers

Copyright Page

© 2026 Darney K. "K Born" Rivers

ISBN

Printed in the United States of America

This is a work of nonfiction. Names and events may have been changed for privacy or clarity.

First Edition

Dedication

To those who shaped me, guided me, and stood by me when the world walked away:

Stretch, Shake, Big Cory, Petey from Baltimore, Shy Sean, Monk from BK, Knox from D.C., Mike Campbell, Tone Loc, Cesar from Ohio, D Love, Trent, Paulio, Chip Whip, and my brother E.

Even though my brother wasn't always around, he taught me lessons that stayed with me. To all my family, friends, and mentors — your wisdom, loyalty, and love have been the backbone of my journey.

And to the communities of the Bronx, South Carolina, and everywhere I've walked — this is for you. May our stories, our struggles, and our victories continue to inspire the next generation.

Acknowledgment

I want to acknowledge the mentors, friends, and family who guided me through every stage

of my life—from Creston Avenue to the Bronx streets, from rooftop studios to community spaces.

Special thanks to my parents, whose discipline and love shaped my values; Uncle Dip, whose

mentorship saved me more than once; my children and grandchildren, who remind me daily

why purpose matters; and all the youth, returning citizens, and community members who

taught me that leadership is not about power, but about service.

Finally, I acknowledge the city of the Bronx itself—the streets, the stories, the challenges,

and the victories—which provided the ultimate classroom for survival, strategy, and purpose

Table of Contents

Chapter 1 – Roots of the Bronx & Early Family Life

Chapter 2 – School Experiences & Peer Interaction

Chapter 3 – Emotional Moments & Loss

Chapter 8 – Answers, Solutions & the Next Generation

Epilogue – Legacy & Grandchildren

Back Matter

Author's Note

The events, people, and experiences shared in this book are drawn from my life in the Bronx, from childhood through adulthood. Some names and identifying details have been changed to protect privacy, and certain timelines have been adjusted for clarity and narrative flow.

This memoir is an honest reflection of survival, struggle, and resilience. It is offered with the hope that readers will find inspiration, guidance, and understanding in the journey of a life shaped by challenges, loyalty, and purpose.

My intent is not to sensationalize hardship, but to honor the lessons learned and the people who shaped me — family, mentors, friends, and even the streets themselves.

While some events may be difficult to read, they are shared with transparency because the truth has power. The streets taught me strategy. Music taught me expression. Family taught me love. And the community taught me the importance of service. Together, these lessons became my path.

To the readers of this memoir: may you find courage in adversity, integrity in decision-making, and purpose in every step you take. And may this story remind you that no matter the obstacles, it is possible to survive, thrive, and give back.

Darney K. "K Born" Rivers

Prologue

The Bronx doesn't forgive easily. It doesn't wait. It tests you the moment you open your eyes, long before you understand the rules. And I opened mine on June 11, 1968, at Women's Hospital in Harlem, a newborn in a city that already had a story for me.

Even before I could speak, the city whispered lessons: the rumble of the subway under my feet, the sirens wailing in the night, the laughter and fights echoing down the block. These sounds became my first teachers, though I wouldn't recognize them as such for many years.

I was born to parents who had migrated from Charleston, South Carolina — carrying discipline, resilience, and pride into the Bronx. My father, quiet and dependable, delivered mail across a city that demanded respect through action. My mother, unwavering and sharp, anchored the household with love and structure. They were my first mentors, my compass, and my safe harbor in a world that wouldn't pause for a child.

From the start, I learned that life in the Bronx was dual-natured: beauty and chaos, love and danger, loyalty and betrayal. My earliest lessons didn't come from classrooms or textbooks. They came from watching, listening, surviving, and understanding that every action carried consequence — a currency far more valuable than money.

By the time I could walk the streets on my own, I was already learning survival, strategy, and character. The city demanded it, and I answered. Music, family, mentors, and the streets themselves became my guides. Every step, every encounter, every observation was recorded in my mind, forming the blueprint for a life that would one day transform survival into service.

This memoir is that journey. It is the story of streets that shaped me, lessons that guided me, and the mission that carried me beyond the Bronx into a life of advocacy, mentorship, and legacy.

Because in the end, the debt society claims never clears—but it can be transformed into purpose, resilience, and the power to uplift others.

Chapter 1, Part 1 — Birth & Family Origins

I was born in 1968, on June 11th, at Harlem Women's Hospital. A newborn doesn't remember much, but the environment leaves an imprint. The smell of antiseptic, the bustle of nurses and visitors, and the faint aroma of pizza drifting from the streets below — those were the first sensory markers of the Bronx in my life. Even then, the energy of the city seemed alive, restless, and relentless. It would follow me my entire life.

My parents were both from Charleston, South Carolina, and so were my two older siblings. My younger sisters and I, however, were born in New York City. Nearly all of my family remained in South Carolina, which meant I grew up without a large extended family nearby. I quickly learned that family is not just inherited — it can be built, chosen, and earned. Friends became my siblings; mentors became my parents' second voices guiding me; the neighborhood became my extended home.

One of the most formative influences in my early life was Uncle Dip. He taught me practical skills and life lessons in ways I couldn't learn in school. He taught me to ride a bike without training wheels, how to roller skate, and even how to save money by walking instead of taking the bus, so we could stretch what my mother gave him for outings to the movies or meals. He'd convince us to walk, then split the money among us while using his share for cigarettes or a little drink. Even at that age, I learned the power of planning, foresight, and making the most of limited resources.

Growing up on the Bronx block, I learned quickly about community dynamics and loyalty. If trouble started on the wrong block, one whistle could bring people running off fire escapes, jumping out of windows, ready to fight. Fights were usually with baseball bats, and if someone pulled one out, the opposing side would yell, "He has a bat!" and chaos would erupt. These lessons, learned in the streets, were as crucial as any I learned in a classroom — they taught me vigilance, respect, and the importance of reading situations carefully.

I often spent hours looking out my parents' bedroom window at 170th and Morris and 170th and College Avenues. I watched people move quickly, shouting and gesturing, and wondered about the reasons behind their behavior. Why were those corners the flashpoints for conflict? Why did people stay outside all night, risking themselves? Why were some targeted and others left alone? Hundreds of questions filled my mind, and these observations sharpened my awareness and curiosity.

Mentorship extended beyond family. My early mentors were my older relatives, but soon the streets themselves taught me lessons — some positive, some cautionary. I learned that leadership, loyalty, and honesty were not abstract ideas; they were practical tools for survival. I understood that a misstep could cost someone respect, money, or even their life.

From these early experiences, I learned that intelligence, observation, and emotional resilience were as important as strength or toughness. Even as a child, I had to navigate multiple worlds: home, family, school, and the streets. Each taught me discipline, strategy, and the value of loyalty. Uncle Dip, my parents, and the community around me laid a foundation that would influence everything I did later — from surviving adolescence and street life, to music, incarceration, and ultimately building a nonprofit to serve the youth.

These years formed the bedrock of my character, resilience, and worldview. I learned that life would not wait for me, that I would need to protect those I loved, and that every decision, no matter how small, carried consequences. Loyalty, responsibility, and careful observation became guiding principles, shaping the person I was to become.

Chapter 1, Part 2 — Neighborhood Lessons & Early Curiosity

By the time I was old enough to understand the rhythms of the streets, I realized the Bronx was a classroom without walls. Every block, every corner, every interaction carried a lesson in survival, loyalty, and awareness. My parents had taught me discipline and morality, but the neighborhood taught me practical consequences. If trouble started on the wrong block, it could escalate quickly. Innocent people could get hurt simply because of the block they lived on. That was a reality I had to accept early: you don't choose the block you're born into, but you do learn how to navigate it.

I was endlessly curious. I would spend hours watching people at the intersections of 170th and Morris and 170th and College Avenues. I observed arguments, hustlers, police, and the bystanders. I wondered about their intentions, their fears, their victories, and their defeats. Why were certain corners hotspots for violence and conflict while others were relatively safe? Why were people out all night, defying exhaustion and danger? These observations sharpened my awareness and taught me how to read a person, a situation, and even predict behavior — skills that would save me countless times later in life.

Growing up, I learned quickly that you could be innocent but still inherit the problems of the block you lived on. I witnessed children and young adults caught in circumstances they didn't create, punished for mere association. This harsh reality became part of my early education in justice, fairness, and human behavior. It forced me to be vigilant, to assess risk, and to choose alliances carefully.

My early curiosity extended beyond the streets. I wanted to understand the patterns of life, of people, and of survival. Observing the older kids and adults taught me about strategy, loyalty, and consequence. I watched those who succeeded and those who failed, learning lessons without having to pay the price firsthand each time. It was a combination of observation, reflection, and instinct that began to form the foundation of my street intelligence.

Even as I navigated the neighborhood, I sought guidance from mentors — first my older family members, then trusted neighbors and community figures who could offer perspective. I learned that mentorship wasn't just about advice; it was about example, presence, and shared experience. Lessons came in many forms: sometimes through words, sometimes through action, and sometimes through consequences that I had to witness to fully understand.

The streets, the block, and my curiosity coalesced into an early understanding that life would not always be fair, but knowledge and awareness could provide a powerful edge. From this, I developed a strong sense of responsibility for myself and those around me. I realized that survival required intelligence, observation, loyalty, and the courage to make choices even when consequences were unclear.

Chapter 1, Part 3 — Early Observations & Curiosity

From a very young age, I was fascinated by the rhythms and patterns of life around me. I would stand by the window in my parents' room for hours, watching the energy on the streets of the Bronx, particularly at 170th and Morris and 170th and College Avenues. These corners were alive with activity — kids running, adults arguing, vendors calling out their goods, and police occasionally patrolling. To a casual observer, it might have seemed chaotic. To me, it was a living lesson in human behavior, conflict, and survival.

I noticed how certain people commanded attention simply by the way they carried themselves. How others fell in line with unspoken rules that dictated respect, loyalty, and dominance. I watched arguments escalate and de-escalate, noticing who intervened and who waited for someone else to act. Every movement, every shout, every glance contained information. My young mind recorded it all.

Questions consumed me. Why were those two corners the hotspots for violence and activity? Why did certain kids become leaders while others became targets? Why did some adults navigate conflicts successfully while others failed? These questions weren't just idle curiosity — they were early lessons in strategy, observation, and situational awareness.

Even as I absorbed the lessons of the street, I maintained a sense of discipline and reflection at home. My mentors, from Unc Dip to older neighborhood figures, taught me that intelligence and foresight could save lives. The streets taught me the consequences of miscalculation, but home taught me the value of patience, preparation, and understanding human nature. I learned that knowledge could be weaponized and that awareness could prevent disasters before they began.

By observing, listening, and reflecting, I began to see patterns. I noticed how alliances formed, how loyalty was tested, and how trust could be earned or lost in a single moment. These early observations became the foundation of my ability to navigate complex situations, not only in the streets but later in music, business, and community leadership.

Even small moments became teaching moments. Watching a child defend a friend from bullying, seeing a vendor negotiate prices with a customer, observing the police handle minor disputes — each incident added to a growing understanding of social structure, risk, and human motivation. I internalized these lessons without even realizing I was building a personal strategy for life.

By the time I reached adolescence, these observations had fused with my innate curiosity, my mentors' guidance, and my family's values. I had developed an early sense of strategy, emotional intelligence, and resilience. These skills would carry me through adolescence, the streets, music, and eventually into the work of advocacy and service.

In reflection, these moments of early observation were the first chapters of my education, far beyond any school or classroom. They taught me to see, to think, and to act with awareness — lessons that remain central to every decision I make.

Chapter 1, Part 4 — Mentorship & Discipline

As I grew older, I began to realize that guidance could come from many places — family, neighbors, friends, and even people who weren't part of my immediate circle. At first, my mentors were my older family members, those who had lived longer and experienced more. They taught me basic principles: respect, responsibility, and the consequences of actions. But as I ventured further into the streets and explored the world beyond home, I encountered another layer of mentorship, one that was often unspoken and sometimes risky.

Some of these mentors led me in the right direction, showing me how to handle myself, read situations, and protect those I cared about. Others, I would later realize, were the blind leading the blind, carrying me down paths that taught me harsh lessons through mistakes. From each interaction, I learned something critical: loyalty and discernment are just as important as guidance.

Unc Dip remained my anchor through this time. He continued to show me practical wisdom: how to move in the world strategically, how to make the most of opportunities, and how to navigate relationships with intelligence and integrity. He emphasized that discipline was not just about punishment or rules, but about self-control, planning, and understanding cause and effect.

School and structured environments also provided mentorship. Certain teachers and staff members recognized my potential and encouraged my curiosity, creativity, and leadership abilities. But even when rules were enforced with discipline — whether through detention, corrective measures, or tough conversations — I learned to respect authority while also developing my own critical thinking. The balance between discipline and freedom shaped my ability to navigate adult decisions later in life.

The streets, however, were a harsher teacher. I learned quickly that loyalty, trust, and courage were the currency of survival. Having a "road dog" — a right-hand companion who could be counted on under any circumstance — was essential. I observed how others navigated conflicts, gained respect, and established hierarchies. Mistakes were costly. Betrayal could be fatal. From these experiences, I absorbed the principle that true mentorship isn't just instruction — it's modeling character, values, and accountability through action.

Music and creative partnerships became another form of mentorship. I partnered with Labru, constantly challenging each other to grow, refine our skills, and push boundaries. These experiences taught me discipline in practice: dedication, persistence, and the importance of constantly sharpening one's abilities. I learned that mentorship could be mutual — that you could learn as much from a peer as from someone older or more experienced.

By the time I reached adolescence, the lessons of mentorship and discipline had coalesced into a personal philosophy: life rewards preparation, foresight, loyalty, and integrity. True mentorship equips a person not only with skills and knowledge but with the ability to navigate challenges, make ethical choices, and lead others responsibly.

This part of my journey reinforced that discipline and mentorship are not separate from survival, growth, or leadership — they are the foundation. Every lesson, every interaction, and every test I faced contributed to the person I would become, laying the groundwork for music, street navigation, advocacy, and leadership in the years to follow.

Chapter 1, Part 5 — Reflections & Foreshadowing

Looking back on my earliest years, I can see how the combination of family, neighborhood, mentors, and personal curiosity shaped every part of me. Those moments — watching the corners of 170th and Morris, learning discipline from Unc Dip, observing the street dynamics, and absorbing lessons from both successes and mistakes — created the foundation of my identity, my resilience, and my worldview.

I learned early that life would never pause for me. Every choice carried consequences, every action had ripple effects, and every lesson had to be internalized if I wanted to survive and thrive. I also learned that loyalty and trust are earned, not freely given, and that integrity is far more valuable than reputation alone. These early experiences were more than memories; they were training grounds for adulthood, preparing me for challenges that would test my courage, intelligence, and moral compass.

Even as a child, I was already seeing patterns of cause and effect, opportunity and risk. I learned that the same streets that could teach violence could also teach strategy. That the same mentors who disciplined could also inspire greatness. That the blocks that felt confining could also nurture creativity, resourcefulness, and community.

These lessons foreshadowed everything that would come next: the music, the struggles, the incarceration, the advocacy, and the leadership. They instilled in me a recognition that my experiences could not only shape my own life but potentially guide others — that the insights I gained from survival, observation, and mentorship could be a roadmap for the next generation.

Reflecting on these early years, I also understood that growth is intentional. Life would throw challenges, losses, and temptations in my path, but the foundation built in the Bronx, with Uncle Dip and the block, gave me a framework for decision-making. It taught me that obstacles could become lessons, that pain could become wisdom, and that survival required both adaptability and moral clarity.

Chapter 1 closes with a quiet but profound truth: the person I am today, and the person I would become tomorrow, is built on the bricks of every block, every mentor, and every observation. Those early experiences were the prologue to a life of challenges, triumphs, mistakes, lessons, and ultimately, service to others. The Bronx gave me roots, and those roots would carry me through every chapter that followed.

The Corner of 170th & Morris

I would watch from my parent's window, seeing the chaos unfold below. Adults yelling, kids running, cops patrolling. I didn't understand why certain kids were singled out, or why fights erupted so quickly. Yet every day, I learned something new — how respect was earned, how loyalty was measured, and how the smallest gesture could turn the tide. These street lessons became the blueprint for everything I did later — in music, in family, and in my community.

SECTION A — ROOTS & ORIGINS

#NeverBeCaged
IAmMyCommunity

Survival, purpose, and identity. This image represents the foundation—who I was becoming before the world decided who I should be.

Bloodline and love. Family is not just who raised you, but who reminds you why you must keep going.

17

I
AM MY
COMMUNITY
IAmMyCommunityInc@gmail.com

Movement and community. Carrying the flag meant carrying responsibility—for those seen and those erased.

Future, love, and continuity. This moment is proof that everything endured still had meaning.

School was always a place of discovery for me, but it was also a battlefield of curiosity, social negotiation, and early lessons in consequences. From the first days at Junior High School 22 on 167th Street and Morris Avenue, I quickly realized that every action, even those taken without full understanding, could have serious outcomes.

In the 4th grade, I went with a few friends to a local junior high after school. One of the kids took a watch from a younger student. I didn't run, and in truth, I barely knew most of the other kids involved. But the next morning, police arrived in our classroom, and I was arrested for the first time in my life. I was not afraid, but I felt a profound shame — it was my mother's birthday, a day that should have been filled with celebration and not handcuffs.

When my mother arrived at the precinct around 7 pm after work, she calmly picked me up. One of the officers suggested she should punish me physically, but she simply shook her head and said: "It's my birthday. If I hit him today, I might end up killing him." That moment wasn't just a memory — it was a lesson in restraint, perspective, and the power of parental love, shaping the way I would respond to crises for the rest of my life.

Even at this young age, I was naturally drawn to people, leadership, and social observation. My mother often warned me, "You're too curious. Don't slow me down. Don't distract others. Keep your eyes open, but don't get lost in the crowd." By the time I was five or six, I had a network of friends older than me, mentors in the neighborhood, and a way of speaking with adults that belied my age. I could spend hours talking, learning, and observing — the first glimmers of my later ability to read people, situations, and systems.

School itself was a mix of structure and improvisation. I loved attending the P.A.L. programs, where teachers like Mrs. Puckerin, Mrs. Smalls/Harris, and Mr. Julius ran classrooms not by age but by ability. Those two classrooms became microcosms of the world: students challenged, tested, and supported each other in ways standard schools could never replicate. Discipline was strict but rooted in care — skipping class, fighting, or misbehaving wasn't just noted; consequences followed swiftly, often in partnership with parents. These experiences ingrained responsibility, respect, and the understanding that every action carries a consequence.

By the time I graduated from the alternative learning space, my reading and math skills were at college level, and I was automatically placed in college-bound classes at Walton High School as a freshman. I had learned to value knowledge, diligence, and the power of learning, seeing early that education was both a shield and a sword in the Bronx.

These early school years were more than academics — they were a laboratory for social intelligence. I learned to navigate peer groups, assert boundaries, and identify mentors. Every challenge, mistake, and success added layers to my understanding of the world. By blending lessons from the classroom with observations from the streets, I was already developing the skills, insight, and foresight that would later define my life.

Chapter 2, Part 2 — Peer Interactions & Social Lessons

From a young age, I realized that people were naturally drawn to me, whether for friendship, guidance, or influence. Even at five or six years old, I had a unique ability to connect with others — adults and children alike. My mother would often warn me before we left the house: "Remember, you have to be careful with the friends you make. Not everyone has your best interests at heart." I listened, but even then, I was already forming networks, building relationships, and learning the delicate balance of trust, loyalty, and influence.

I was probably the only five-year-old who had adult friends I could converse with for hours, play cards with, and learn from. These early interactions taught me more than school ever could. I learned how to read people, how to gauge intentions, and how to navigate social hierarchies. These skills became a cornerstone of my survival — both in the streets and in life.

Friendships were not just about play or fun; they were lessons in loyalty and accountability. I saw how some kids broke trust, how others held their word, and how a single act could elevate or ruin a reputation. This understanding guided me in choosing allies and mentors carefully, knowing that a reliable companion could make the difference between success and failure, safety and danger.

School trips, playground disputes, and casual interactions all became teaching moments. I learned early that observation and reflection were as critical as participation. Watching others make mistakes, succeed, or face consequences allowed me to internalize lessons without paying the full price myself. I began to understand the unspoken rules that governed social interactions, community respect, and influence — lessons I would carry throughout my life.

Even mundane experiences, like going for haircuts or running errands, were opportunities to observe social behavior and understand how trust, respect, and communication shaped relationships. My ability to connect, listen, and learn from these small moments built a foundation for leadership, problem-solving, and empathy.

By the time I was in middle school, these early peer interactions had taught me that influence, guidance, and loyalty were interdependent. You could lead, but only if you understood the people around you. You could trust, but only if you discerned intentions clearly. And you could survive — even thrive — only if you mastered both observation and action.

These lessons weren't abstract theories; they were hard-earned wisdom from living in a community where choices had immediate and real consequences. They became the blueprint for navigating adolescence, confronting street challenges, and later shaping my approach to music, entrepreneurship, and community leadership.

Chapter 2, Part 3 — Academic Growth & Alternative Learning

While my peers often struggled to see the value in school, I found learning to be both a challenge and a sanctuary. I thrived in the alternative learning space, where instruction wasn't based strictly on age but on ability. Teachers like Mrs. Puckerin, Mrs. Smalls/Harris, and Mr. Julius created classrooms that felt more like workshops than schools — a place where curiosity, intelligence, and ambition could flourish.

Classes were intimate, with only a handful of students per room. Lessons were tailored to each student's pace, and discipline was rooted in care and accountability. Skipping school, fighting with classmates, or misbehaving didn't just lead to a lecture; it led to swift action. Teachers and staff — often in collaboration with parents — would ensure that the lesson was internalized. Sometimes that meant a firm hand or a tough conversation, but it always came with love and guidance. I personally experienced a few of these corrective moments, and while painful at the time, they left lasting lessons about responsibility and the consequences of choices.

Beyond the academics, this environment fostered emotional intelligence and self-discipline. Students were encouraged to explore, question, and reflect. I learned how to manage frustration, build resilience, and maintain focus under pressure. These lessons weren't just about schoolwork; they were preparing me for life, teaching me that intelligence alone wasn't enough — you needed emotional and strategic awareness to survive and thrive.

By the time I graduated from the alternative learning space, my reading and math skills were college-level, which earned me automatic placement in college-bound classes at Walton High School as a freshman. I had internalized the value of education: not just as a pathway to opportunity, but as a form of protection and empowerment. The skills I developed in these early academic settings — observation, discipline, and perseverance — became tools I would later use in the streets, music, and community leadership.

This phase of my life also revealed the importance of mentorship within structured environments. The teachers and staff were more than educators — they were guides, role models, and pillars of accountability. Their belief in my potential shaped my confidence, while their insistence on responsibility shaped my character.

Looking back, I see that the alternative learning space wasn't just a school; it was a laboratory for life, teaching lessons about adaptability, focus, collaboration, and strategy. It was where I learned that success requires a balance of knowledge, discipline, and observation — lessons that would echo throughout my adolescent and adult life.

Chapter 2, Part 4 — Peer Challenges & Social Navigation

Navigating friendships and peer groups in the Bronx was as much a lesson in survival as any classroom. From a very young age, I realized that who you surrounded yourself with could determine not only your reputation but your safety and opportunities. My mother often warned me, "Choose your friends wisely — you become like the people you spend the most time with." She was right.

Even as a five- or six-year-old, I had the rare ability to attract peers from all walks of life. Some were older, some younger, some more experienced in the streets, and some just curious about the world like me. I could spend hours talking to them, learning their routines, their habits, and their tricks for navigating the city. Unlike most kids, I wasn't scared of adults or older teens. I learned early that respect and awareness could give you access to knowledge and safety that many others lacked.

In schoolyards, streets, and playgrounds, I honed the skill of reading people. Every conversation, every gesture, and every tone carried meaning. I learned who could be trusted, who was unpredictable, and who was simply seeking an opportunity to exploit someone. These observations weren't about cynicism — they were about survival, awareness, and building networks that could help me and protect me.

Peer challenges weren't always verbal; sometimes they were physical. Fights broke out over territory, respect, or misunderstandings. But there was also a competitive camaraderie — a testing ground to sharpen instincts, resilience, and strategy. I learned when to step up, when to step back, and how to negotiate without losing respect. Some friends became lifelong allies; others were fleeting, teaching temporary lessons in trust and betrayal.

Social navigation extended beyond the street and school walls. I discovered that every interaction was an opportunity to learn or teach, to expand influence, and to create leverage for myself. Simple activities — walking to the store, attending a birthday party, or even just playing cards — became lessons in observation, negotiation, and communication. I practiced diplomacy with my peers, learned to mediate conflicts, and understood the subtle power of influence and persuasion at an early age.

Even in fun or playful moments, I was conscious of reputation and perception. I noticed that peers, teachers, and even strangers assigned value based on actions, consistency, and integrity. If someone broke their word or acted out of selfishness, word would travel fast. By observing these dynamics, I built a framework for trust and loyalty that would later shape my approach to music collaborations, community leadership, and mentorship.

The cumulative effect of these experiences was a keen sense of social intelligence, far beyond what most children develop naturally. I learned how to read situations, anticipate reactions, and protect myself emotionally and physically. The

Bronx streets were my training ground, and the lessons I learned about friendship, loyalty, and discernment became the foundation for all my later successes.

Chapter 2, Part 5 — Lessons Learned & Reflections

Looking back on my early school years and neighborhood life, I realize that every experience was a lesson — often hard, sometimes painful, but always valuable. The arrests, the run-ins with authority, the conflicts with peers, and the triumphs in classrooms and on the streets weren't isolated events; they were all part of a larger education in resilience, responsibility, and strategy.

One of the biggest lessons I learned was accountability. Actions had consequences, whether immediate or delayed. When the police came to arrest me in fourth grade, or when disputes erupted over territory or respect, I understood that my choices directly influenced outcomes for myself and for others around me. It wasn't enough to react impulsively; I had to think, calculate, and anticipate the consequences of my actions.

Another lesson was the value of observation. Watching how older kids interacted, how teachers disciplined, and how neighbors responded to incidents gave me an informal education in human behavior. I learned to read expressions, tone, and body language. I saw how respect was earned, how fear could be manipulated, and how loyalty could be cultivated or broken. These lessons weren't taught in school, but they were more impactful than anything I learned from textbooks.

I also discovered the importance of adaptability. Life on the block and in school didn't follow a script. Situations changed rapidly — friends switched sides, new rules emerged in the neighborhood, and authority figures acted unpredictably. I learned to adapt quickly, to adjust strategies, and to stay focused on my goals even when circumstances were chaotic or unfair.

Equally critical was the lesson of empathy and influence. I realized that leadership wasn't about physical strength or intimidation alone. It was about understanding others, anticipating their needs and motivations, and helping guide them toward better outcomes. Whether mediating disputes among peers or mentoring younger kids on the block, I learned that influence was a tool far more powerful than brute force.

Perhaps the most enduring lesson from this time was the value of preparation and planning for the future. While other kids focused solely on the moment, I was already thinking about how experiences today would shape tomorrow. How could I use knowledge gained from missteps to avoid larger pitfalls later? How could I transform small victories into larger opportunities? This mindset became the foundation for everything I did in later life — from navigating the music industry to building my nonprofit and mentoring youth.

Reflecting on these experiences, I understand now that these early years were the crucible in which my character was forged. The streets, the schools, the peer dynamics — they were all shaping me into someone who could not only survive adversity but thrive in it. Every challenge taught resilience, every success instilled confidence, and every mistake provided a roadmap for future decisions.

Chapter 2 wasn't just about surviving childhood in the Bronx; it was about learning how to live with intention, strategy, and integrity, laying the groundwork for everything that came after. These lessons became my compass, guiding me through the complexities of adolescence, young adulthood, and ultimately, my career, my family life, and my work in the community.

Chapter 3, Part 1 — Emotional Loss & Early Trauma

The first time I truly felt the weight of loss was when my mother passed away. For years afterward, I carried a grief so heavy it felt like a physical burden. I didn't seek death by suicide, but I often found myself walking paths of extreme risk, testing boundaries, and putting myself in dangerous situations as if I were daring fate. I remember days when I was caught in two or three shootouts — separate conflicts, different people, different motives — yet they all had one shared goal: to end me.

People around me called me reckless, fearless, a "one-man gang," or even crazy. But none of them saw the emotional storm inside me. Every fight, every confrontation, every night spent wandering the streets was my way of coping with a heart shattered by loss and a mind consumed by grief. On the outside, I projected confidence, skill, and control. On the inside, I was navigating a storm that few could understand.

This period taught me resilience in its rawest form. Survival was no longer optional; it was the only path forward. I learned to calculate risk, observe human behavior, and trust only those who had proven themselves through action. The streets became a school where the lessons were cruel but necessary.

At the same time, I internalized the immense value of a person's word. I saw that honesty and trust could create opportunities even in the most chaotic circumstances. Someone keeping their word could get more credit, respect, and trust than someone with money in hand. Conversely, betrayal could be deadly. I watched lives unravel and reputations destroyed because someone broke their word. I understood that in life, the integrity of your word could mean the difference between freedom and a casket.

Even in the darkest moments, I began to notice small threads of guidance and protection from people who cared, quietly influencing my choices without preaching. These individuals showed me that even in chaos, loyalty and guidance can exist, and sometimes, that guidance saves a life more effectively than any rule, lecture, or punishment.

Chapter 3, Part 2 — Losing My Father & Lessons from Grief

When I was incarcerated in 1992, the world delivered a blow I wasn't prepared for — my father passed away. The pain was immediate and deep, cutting to the core of my being. He wasn't just a parent; he was the man who gave me life, who had quietly shaped my understanding of strength, loyalty, and responsibility. Yet, I wasn't there for him in his final moments.

I had spoken to him often on the phone, but I longed to be physically present. I wanted to see his face, to feel his hand, to share those final breaths. Instead, I was confined to a cell, helpless and powerless. It was a crushing lesson in the reality that time doesn't wait for anyone, a lesson in loss that no conversation or phone call could remedy.

Escorted by a correctional officer to his funeral, I realized the depth of my own responsibility for my life. I had put myself in a position where I could not be there for the man who had always been there for me. That experience ignited a determination that would guide every decision I made afterward: I would never again allow my choices to rob me of precious moments with those I loved.

The grief taught me another vital lesson: life is fragile, and opportunities are fleeting. I had to move through the world with intentionality, to cherish every moment with family and friends, and to create a life that honored the sacrifices of those who came before me. The streets, the incarceration, and the chaos of my early life had given me resilience, but this loss added a layer of profound emotional clarity — a recognition that some lessons could only come through pain, and some wisdom only through grief.

In those moments, I began to see patterns I had ignored before. I understood that life wasn't just about survival in the streets or excelling academically; it was about leaving a legacy, honoring those who built you, and preparing yourself for the future. The experiences of loss taught me empathy, patience, and the responsibility that comes with leadership — lessons that would carry through my music, my family life, and eventually, my work in the community.

This chapter of my life wasn't just about sorrow; it was about reflection, growth, and the internalization of lessons that would shape my choices for decades. Losing my father while I was behind bars crystallized the importance of presence, the urgency of love, and the unspoken promise I made to myself: to live a life worthy of the sacrifices, guidance, and example he had given me.

Chapter 3, Part 3 — Survival, Street Lessons & Early Incarceration

After losing both of my parents, the streets became my sanctuary and my battlefield. Life had already taught me the art of survival, but this chapter of my youth tested every lesson I had ever learned. Every day, I walked a line between resilience and recklessness, between risk and instinct, and I remember standing alone on the block, hearing the shots, feeling the emptiness. Why her? Why now? I asked myself. But I also knew I couldn't fall apart — I had to keep moving. Each step, each decision, was a chance to honor her memory. I whispered under my breath, "I'll make this work. I'll survive. I'll turn this pain into something bigger than me." between loyalty and self-preservation.

I remember vividly the sense of invincibility mixed with despair. Shootouts, fights, and confrontations were no longer sporadic; they became the rhythm of daily existence. Yet, beneath the chaos, I was learning the true meaning of consequences. Every action could result in freedom or a casket, every choice could build opportunity or destruction.

Despite the constant danger, I sought structure in the madness. My father's absence was a void that I attempted to fill with discipline — a relentless self-imposed accountability. I realized that trust and loyalty were the most valuable currency on these streets. One mistake, one broken promise, and everything could crumble. I learned early that a man's word wasn't just reputation — it was survival.

Being incarcerated taught me lessons I would carry for life. In 1992, during one of my first serious incarcerations, I witnessed firsthand how the system could strip a man of freedom, dignity, and connection. Rikers Island wasn't just a place of confinement; it was a crucible for reflection. I watched how men reacted to injustice, how some hardened themselves into bitterness while others found clarity in restraint.

I also discovered that leadership isn't assigned — it's proven. Even in the chaos of prison life, respect had to be earned through consistent action, integrity, and the courage to stand for what was right. I observed mentors, peers, and even adversaries, learning to navigate power structures with strategy rather than aggression alone.

Music and creativity became my lifeline. I poured my experiences into lyrics, crafting narratives that reflected the struggle, resilience, and aspirations of a young man growing up in the Bronx. Songs weren't just entertainment; they were declarations of survival, statements of identity, and vessels for emotion I couldn't otherwise express.

Ultimately, this period of my life cemented a philosophy that would guide me for decades: life is defined not by the challenges you face, but by how you respond to them. Street lessons, personal losses, and early encounters with the justice system taught me that survival requires vision, strategy, loyalty, and self-respect — and that those who endure with integrity leave behind a legacy far greater than any material gain.

Chapter 3, Part 4 — Reflections & Lessons Learned

Looking back on those turbulent years, I see that the streets, the early incarcerations, and the constant threats weren't just random trials — they were lessons in resilience, strategy, and morality. Each encounter taught me to read people, assess risk, and navigate situations with clarity. Every close call underscored the importance of foresight, patience, and the ability to stay calm under pressure.

I also learned that survival requires more than physical skill. Mental acuity, emotional intelligence, and strategic thinking were just as important as knowing how to defend oneself or maneuver through a fight. I realized that observing patterns, understanding motivations, and predicting outcomes could prevent harm far more effectively than brute force alone.

Perhaps the most critical lesson was about loyalty and trust. Street life might glorify independence and rebellion, but I discovered that success and safety were built on the foundation of dependable allies. A single trustworthy companion could be the difference between life and death, between success and ruin. That bond had to be nurtured with consistency, respect, and honesty — values that would later influence how I built relationships in music, business, and community work.

During this period, I also reflected on the power of words and promises. I witnessed how quickly reputations could be shattered, how betrayal could escalate violence, and how a broken promise could destroy more than just trust — it could destroy lives. Conversely, keeping one's word became a sacred form of currency, opening doors and creating opportunities where money alone could not.

These reflections shaped my approach to life in every domain: family, friendships, music, and eventually my nonprofit work. I learned that adversity could refine character, that trauma could teach empathy, and that mistakes, if analyzed and internalized, could become guiding principles.

Chapter 3, Part 5 — Transition into Young Adulthood & Turning Points

As I moved into my late teens and early twenties, the lessons of childhood and adolescence collided with the realities of adulthood. The streets, once a training ground, became a proving ground, and the choices I made would reverberate far beyond my immediate world. The losses I had endured, the arrests I had faced, and the close calls I had survived all converged into a single, undeniable truth: life demanded responsibility, foresight, and resilience.

The death of my father and the absence of my mother left a void that no adult supervision could fill. I had to learn quickly how to navigate complex social dynamics, manage risk, and assume a level of accountability far beyond my years. Every encounter on the streets, every altercation, and every strategic decision shaped me. I understood that survival required both instinct and intellect, and that those who failed to recognize the balance often fell victim to chaos.

During this time, music became more than an outlet — it became a lifeline. My partner Labru and I honed our skills daily, competing and collaborating in ways that sharpened both creativity and discipline. We battled at talent shows, wrote and rewrote lyrics until every line resonated, and learned to translate our life experiences into art. These moments weren't just performances; they were lessons in focus, resilience, and the power of storytelling. Every verse, every rhyme, was a reflection of our struggles, our triumphs, and the streets that had shaped us.

The streets themselves continued to teach — lessons in loyalty, trust, and consequence. I learned to identify true allies from opportunists, to anticipate danger before it arrived, and to act with clarity under pressure. Even the smallest interactions — sharing a meal, negotiating a deal, or mediating a dispute — became microcosms of life lessons in strategy, leadership, and human behavior.

Equally important were the internal transformations. I began
to develop foresight, purpose, and vision, understanding that
the choices I made today would define the man I became
tomorrow. I learned that strength was not only measured by
physical prowess or fearlessness, but by the capacity to
endure hardship with integrity, to act with intention, and to
protect those who relied on you.

Looking back, these turning points laid the foundation for
everything that followed: my music career, my entrepreneurial
ventures, my advocacy work, and ultimately the creation of
my nonprofit, I Am My Community Inc. Each challenge, each
victory, each heartbreak, was part of a larger narrative about
growth, resilience, and the pursuit of purpose.

Chapter 3 closes with the understanding that young adulthood is not merely a stage of age, but a test of character. The streets, the losses, the early brushes with the justice system, and the triumphs in music all converged to forge a young man who would not only survive but begin to thrive — prepared to step into leadership, community service, and the long arc of life that awaited them.

Chapter 4, Part 1 — Street Encounters & Early Survival

As I stepped further into young adulthood, the streets became more than a backdrop — they were the stage where I learned the laws of loyalty, respect, and survival. Every corner, every block, every encounter carried lessons that no classroom could teach. From a young age, I had understood that having a trusted sidekick was essential. Someone who could move with you, cover your back, and share the burden of risk. Labru was that person for me. We were inseparable, bonded by trust, shared experience, and a mutual understanding that loyalty was non-negotiable.

Every day with Labru was a lesson in discipline and competitive excellence. We battled each other in rap contests not just for money, but to sharpen our craft. Music became our arena for testing skills, creativity, and resilience. One evening at the world-famous Disco Fever in the Bronx, I won first place while Labru came in second. That night, as we split the prize money, we were observed by DJ Starchild, who would later introduce us to a network that connected us to Teddy Riley and Gusto Wells — a pivotal moment that transformed our music trajectory.

But survival wasn't only about music. It was about understanding the unspoken rules of the streets. I learned that being a hustler meant more than selling product; it meant honoring your word, planning ahead, and building strategies for both immediate gain and long-term stability. Many so-called hustlers around me ended up broke, not because of lack of skill, but because they failed to plan, failed to honor commitments, and failed to think beyond the moment. Real hustling required vision.

I also learned early that danger could come from any direction. Conflicts arose unexpectedly, alliances shifted, and authority figures were often unpredictable. These experiences demanded not only physical skill but mental acuity and strategic thinking. I observed, calculated, and adapted constantly. Every interaction — whether a dispute over respect, a negotiation for resources, or a clash of rival groups — was a test of judgment and foresight.

The streets also reinforced the value of mentorship and guidance. Older figures, experienced in both the harsh realities of urban life and the complexities of human behavior, served as informal teachers. They offered insights, cautionary tales, and wisdom that, while hard-earned, became invaluable tools for navigating both music and life. I realized that knowledge and experience could be leveraged as a weapon and a shield — sometimes even more powerful than physical force.

Ultimately, these street encounters were more than just survival exercises; they were training in leadership, resilience, and strategic thinking. They prepared me for the responsibilities I would later take on in music, in community work, and in my personal life. Each challenge faced and each obstacle overcome was a lesson in self-reliance, the importance of relationships, and the value of integrity in a world where trust was scarce.

Chapter 4, Part 2 — Music, Mentorship & Rising Opportunities

While the streets taught lessons in survival and strategy, music became my compass, guiding me through chaos toward something purposeful. Labru and I spent countless hours writing, rehearsing, and battling — not just for victory in the moment, but to sharpen our skills for the opportunities that awaited. Each rhyme, each verse, and each freestyle was a test of creativity, discipline, and focus.

Our first major breakthrough came at Disco Fever, a legendary Bronx venue where talent was showcased and reputations were forged. Winning first place in a talent contest, with Labru following closely behind, was more than just a prize — it was validation. DJ Starchild noticed our potential and connected us to the larger network of artists and producers, ultimately introducing us to D.J. Brucie B, Teddy Riley, and Gusto Wells. These connections marked a pivotal turning point, bridging street credibility with professional opportunity.

Mentorship played an essential role in our journey. Teddy Riley, already pioneering the New Jack Swing movement, didn't just provide production expertise — he became a teacher, showing us how to structure songs, arrange harmonies, and convey stories through music. With each session in the studio, I internalized not just technical skills, but lessons in professionalism, collaboration, and creative integrity.

Beyond music, mentorship included lessons in business and strategy. Labru and I were shown the importance of branding, presentation, and networking. The streets had taught us loyalty and trust, but the music industry required negotiation, foresight, and long-term planning. These lessons would become invaluable as we navigated record deals, endorsements, and promotional opportunities.

During this period, I also began to understand the importance of balancing ambition with responsibility. Music offered the promise of fame and financial reward, but it also demanded time, focus, and dedication. Each decision — which gigs to take, which collaborators to trust, and how to present ourselves — carried consequences that could either propel us forward or hinder our progress. The discipline we learned in school and on the streets became critical to making smart, sustainable choices.

The Recording Studio Moment

The smell of fresh vinyl, the hum of the mixing board — I could feel the pulse of every beat. Labru and I locked eyes, silently daring each other to bring our best. This wasn't just about winning a talent show anymore; it was about staking our claim, making a mark, leaving a legacy. Every note, every lyric, carried the weight of my upbringing, my struggles, and my dreams.

Finally, the opportunities we seized were amplified by the systems and structures we built. We documented lyrics, rehearsed regularly, and maintained a schedule that mirrored professional expectations. This approach allowed us to scale our impact, prepare for performances, and consistently deliver quality work. It taught me that success is rarely accidental — it is constructed through careful planning, mentorship, and deliberate action.

Music became more than a career pathway — it became a framework for growth, mentorship, and leadership. It was proof that lessons from the streets, family, and peers could converge to create a life with purpose, direction, and opportunity. Chapter 4 was not just about surviving young adulthood; it was about leveraging talent, relationships, and discipline to carve out a path for the future.

Chapter 4, Part 3 — Hustling, Risk, and Strategic Thinking

Life on the streets was never simple. Every day brought opportunities, challenges, and decisions that could define your path — sometimes for years to come. I quickly realized that hustling was more than moving product or making money; it was an exercise in strategy, trust, and long-term planning.

From my earliest experiences, I understood that success required discipline and foresight. The streets rewarded those who honored commitments, anticipated challenges, and built relationships wisely. A man's word was currency — more valuable than cash in the pocket — because reputation and trust determined whether you survived and thrived.

I also discovered that hustling was a game of scaling opportunities while minimizing risk. Observing peers and rivals, I learned that many who called themselves "hustlers" were actually short-term operators — individuals who worked without a plan, consumed gains recklessly, and ultimately failed. A real hustler measured the long-term impact of each move, built networks carefully, and invested in skills, relationships, and opportunities that could compound over time.

Labru and I applied these lessons not just to street business but also to music. Every performance, every battle, every recording session was a negotiation in strategy. We learned to maximize opportunities, divide resources effectively, and capitalize on timing. The discipline and intelligence required to navigate the streets translated directly into how we approached music, business, and life.

Risk management became a core part of my identity. Whether handling conflict on a corner or negotiating a deal in the studio, I learned to assess every situation for threats, advantages, and potential outcomes. Survival wasn't about avoiding risk entirely — it was about controlling risk, making calculated moves, and knowing when to act or wait.

Beyond strategy and money, I absorbed the importance of mentorship and example. Younger kids on the block watched how Labru and I conducted ourselves, learning about integrity, decision-making, and the consequences of actions. Hustling, for me, was about more than profit; it was teaching leadership, responsibility, and foresight by example.

These lessons shaped the foundation for later stages of my life: the music industry, entrepreneurial ventures, and eventually, my work with I Am My Community Inc. Chapter 4, Part 3 reminds me that every decision carries weight, and the principles learned during these formative years — strategy, trust, risk assessment, and mentorship — would guide me through adulthood and help me build lasting impact.

Chapter 4, Part 4 — Music, Legacy, and Community Lessons

By the time we were recording New Generation with Teddy Riley and Gusto Wells, I began to understand that music was far more than entertainment — it was a tool to express, influence, and uplift. The streets had taught me survival, strategy, and loyalty, but music taught me voice, vision, and the power of storytelling. Every lyric we wrote reflected experiences that were raw, real, and rooted in the realities of Bronx life: the struggles, the triumphs, the heartbreak, and the hope.

The process of creating music was itself an education in discipline, patience, and collaboration. We spent hours in the studio, perfecting verses, harmonies, and flows. Each session required focus, creativity, and a willingness to be challenged. Teddy Riley, a master of the New Jack Swing sound, demanded precision but also encouraged experimentation. He taught me that innovation requires both skill and fearless authenticity.

Beyond technical mastery, music offered lessons in legacy and influence. I realized that what we created could inspire, provoke thought, and even guide others. Songs weren't just personal victories; they were tools for shaping community perception and identity. This understanding sparked a larger awareness: every action, every decision, every word carries weight — whether on the streets, in the studio, or in the community.

I also began to see the role of mentorship and giving back. As we gained recognition, younger artists looked to us as examples. Labru and I made it a priority to support aspiring musicians, guide peers, and share knowledge that could help them navigate both the industry and life. It wasn't about fame or money; it was about responsibility, influence, and building a foundation for others to thrive.

The experience of music taught me about legacy beyond personal achievement. Success isn't measured solely by accolades or wealth, but by the impact one leaves on people, culture, and community. This perspective would later inform how I structured my nonprofit, I Am My Community Inc, ensuring that programs for youth were rooted in lessons of integrity, opportunity, and empowerment.

Finally, this period reinforced a truth I had learned early on the streets: structure and systems amplify impact. Whether in music, business, or community service, creating frameworks that endure beyond individual effort is key. Every mentorship program, every workshop, and every initiative we built became a blueprint for sustained positive influence — a lesson that would carry me into the next chapters of life, where advocacy and service became central to my purpose.

Chapter 4, Part 5 — Reflections & Foreshadowing: Laying the Groundwork for Service & Advocacy

Looking back on this period, I can see how the lessons of streets, survival, and music converged to prepare me for a larger purpose. It wasn't enough to survive or even to thrive personally — I realized that true impact required giving back, building structures, and leading with intention. Every challenge, every close call, and every milestone in music contributed to a blueprint for service that would guide my later work with youth and my community.

The streets had taught me the hard truths of loyalty, trust, and consequence. Music had taught me the power of voice, discipline, and vision. Together, these experiences instilled an understanding that real leadership is not self-serving — it is about creating opportunities for others to rise. I began to think not just about my path, but about how I could influence the next generation, how I could turn experiences of hardship into tools for empowerment.

Reflections during this period also emphasized the importance of systems and consistency. I understood that individual actions, while meaningful, were limited in scope. Lasting change required structures — programs that could operate independently, mentorship systems that could reach beyond my immediate presence, and processes that could scale without losing integrity. This foresight would become essential when establishing I Am My Community Inc, ensuring that youth could benefit from consistent guidance, resources, and support regardless of my direct involvement.

Foreshadowing the next chapter, these lessons formed the foundation for service, advocacy, and leadership. The streets, music, and survival strategies had all been practice for something bigger: designing a life that could transform communities, empower youth, and provide alternatives to cycles of violence and neglect. Every decision in this period — from how I built my network in music to how I mentored peers — was laying groundwork for the chapters ahead, where advocacy would become as central to my identity as survival had been.

Ultimately, Chapter 4 closes with the understanding that preparation meets opportunity. The lessons learned — loyalty, strategy, mentorship, and systems thinking — were all precursors to a life dedicated not just to personal achievement, but to lifting others and building sustainable impact. The streets, the studios, and the challenges had equipped me to step confidently into a role as a guide, a mentor, and a leader for the generations that would follow.

SECTION B — MOVEMENT & LEGACY

Presence and proof. This moment documents survival turned into visibility.

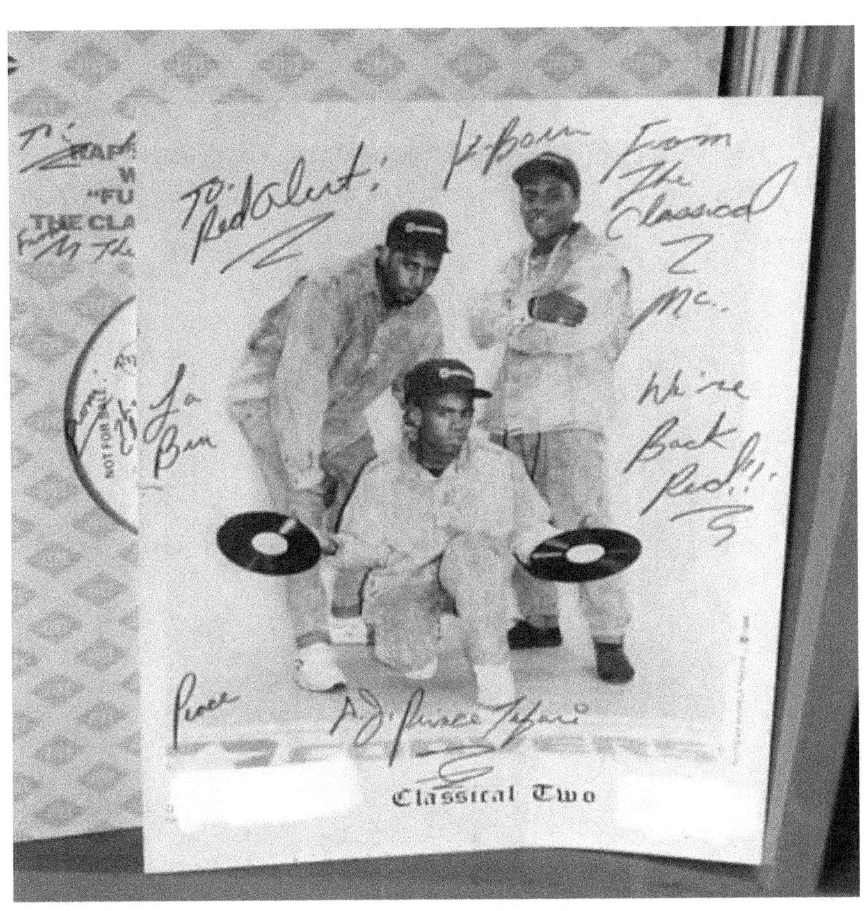
To Red Alert:
La Bam
Peace
DJ Prince Johari
From The Classical 2 MC.
We're Back Red!!
Classical Two

Legacy in motion. What we build in the streets echoes far beyond them.

History remembered. This image captures work that could not be erased.

58

Continuity. The past standing beside the present, unbroken.

A Note for the Next Generation

Dear Ones,

Life will try to knock you down before you even know how to walk. But remember: every setback is a lesson. Loyalty, respect, and accountability are your foundation. If you ever lose your way, look back at the people who have guided you and the lessons they've taught. And know that your actions — small or large — ripple far beyond what you see

Chapter 5, Part 1 — Daily Routines, Discipline, and Values

Once I became a father, my daily life shifted into a rhythm of responsibility that far surpassed anything I had known on the streets or in the studio. Each morning began with getting my children ready for school, ensuring they were nourished, prepared, and mentally ready for the day ahead. This routine was not just a duty — it was a lesson in consistency, accountability, and intentionality. My actions were not for me alone; they modeled behavior, instilled values, and created a standard that my children could emulate.

I taught them early that association shapes identity. Hanging out with peers who lacked ambition or integrity would naturally pull them into similar patterns. Conversely, surrounding oneself with disciplined, motivated, and trustworthy people opened doors, fostered growth, and instilled confidence. From a young age, my children understood that success required both effort and selective association — lessons I had painfully learned through my own trials on the streets.

The responsibilities of fatherhood were compounded by the lessons I had learned in school, music, and survival. I stressed education as non-negotiable, emphasizing that they could leverage knowledge in ways I wished I had at their age. While I had been arrested over 77 times, I made it clear that there was no need for them to repeat my mistakes — their path could be measured, disciplined, and purposeful. I taught them to ask questions, seek knowledge, and respect their own potential, regardless of the obstacles that life might place in their way.

Rules in our home were clear and uncompromising. No drugs, no cigarettes, no tolerance for behaviors that would compromise integrity or safety. These weren't just household rules; they were the foundation for a moral framework. My family and friends knew these boundaries, so there was no confusion or conflict. Boundaries like these created security, accountability, and an environment where values were taught through both example and expectation.

Beyond logistics and rules, I sought to impart the larger lessons of resilience, emotional intelligence, and foresight. Fatherhood demanded reflection, patience, and strategic thinking. I wanted my children to understand the consequences of decisions, the importance of loyalty, and the value of integrity — lessons I had internalized in music, on the streets, and during periods of hardship.

Even as a teenager myself when my first daughter was born, I embraced responsibility. Early fatherhood accelerated my growth, forcing me to balance ambition, survival, and love, and to transform life experiences into actionable wisdom. Each moment — from packing lunches to attending school events, from bedtime stories to real conversations about choices and consequences — reinforced a core principle: discipline and love are inseparable in building character and preparing for the world.

Chapter 5, Part 2 — Parenting Challenges & Street Wisdom

Parenting in the Bronx was never just about feeding, clothing, or transporting children. It was about teaching resilience in the face of systemic obstacles, instilling morality in a world that often rewarded shortcuts, and preparing young minds for the harsh realities that existed beyond the classroom and the front door. I wanted my children to navigate the streets safely, not by avoiding life, but by understanding it — by learning strategy, awareness, and integrity.

My experiences as a young man gave me perspective. I knew how the wrong environment, careless friendships, or even a single lapse in judgment could lead to disastrous outcomes. When my kids asked questions about the world, I didn't shield them from truth; I shared stories and lessons. I told them about the consequences of poor choices, about loyalty and betrayal, and about the importance of honor even when no one was watching. Every anecdote became a teaching moment, turning memories of risk, survival, and mistakes into wisdom for them.

Balancing fatherhood and community responsibility meant sacrifices and calculations. Every time I took a child to a school event or a community program, I weighed the benefits of exposure, mentorship, and guidance against the unpredictable dangers of the streets. But I refused to let fear dictate our experiences. I believed that courage guided by knowledge created stronger children, capable of making their own informed decisions while retaining respect for rules, safety, and community.

Incorporating street wisdom into parenting meant I was honest about danger. I explained how alliances worked, why trust is precious, and why a person's word is more valuable than gold or cash. I taught them that the streets could be navigated safely if one observed patterns, respected rules, and aligned with trustworthy allies. These were not lessons to instill fear but to empower them with clarity and foresight.

Discipline in our household extended beyond rules. It was about accountability, reflection, and planning. When a child made a mistake, I didn't simply punish; I guided them to understand the implications, correct behavior, and make better decisions next time. Each lesson reinforced the principle that responsibility is not just a duty but a practice of character, and that every choice carries weight in shaping life's trajectory.

Parenting was also about modeling resilience. I demonstrated how to rise after failure, take ownership of mistakes, and remain focused under pressure. From managing daily routines to handling conflicts with patience and strategy, my children observed actions paired with principles — lessons I hoped would stick long after childhood.

Chapter 5, Part 3 — Teaching Values Through Daily Actions

Parenting is not a set of abstract lessons; it is lived experience, repeated day after day, in every small choice, gesture, and moment of presence. I wanted my children to understand values through observation and repetition, not just through words. Every morning when I helped them get ready for school, every homework session, every conversation on the way to appointments became an opportunity to embed principles of responsibility, respect, and accountability.

I stressed the importance of self-discipline early on. Whether it was managing time, saving money, or completing tasks without being reminded, these were small habits that compounded into life-long skills. I taught them to understand cause and effect: if they skipped a responsibility, there would be consequences; if they honored commitments, they would earn trust and opportunities. Lessons were consistent and tangible, grounded in the realities of life I had lived.

But discipline alone wasn't enough. I wanted my children to internalize respect and empathy. Respect for elders, peers, and even those they might disagree with. Empathy for those struggling or in need. I encouraged them to observe not only their own actions but the effect those actions had on others, and to recognize that true strength came not from dominance or intimidation, but from compassion, fairness, and integrity.

Street lessons also shaped how I approached these teachings. I shared stories of loyalty, betrayal, and survival, not to glorify danger but to illustrate the real consequences of choices. I explained how a single misstep, a broken promise, or an unwise association could escalate quickly, sometimes with lifelong consequences. Conversely, I showed how a commitment to honesty, fairness, and follow-through could open doors that money alone could not.

Music and creative expression became tools for teaching as well. I encouraged my children to write, rap, or tell stories about their experiences and observations. Through these outlets, they practiced self-reflection, communication, and problem-solving, turning daily experiences into lessons in personal development. I emphasized that every story, every verse, and every word had power — and that they could choose to use that power to inspire, educate, or uplift others, just as I had learned to do in my own youth.

I also taught financial literacy and planning. From splitting allowances to understanding how to save for future goals, I wanted my children to recognize that money, while necessary, is a tool — not an end. The principles of budgeting, investing in education, and preparing for opportunities were habits designed to give them independence and stability, lessons I had learned painfully in my own life.

Ultimately, Chapter 5, Part 3 is about modeling values consistently, with presence, patience, and intentionality. It is about showing through action that integrity, discipline, empathy, and foresight are not abstract ideas, but practices woven into daily life. By embedding these lessons in routine, observation, and example, I ensured that my children could navigate the world with confidence, wisdom, and resilience, carrying forward principles that I had lived, learned, and refined through years of experience.

Chapter 5, Part 4 — Reflection & Foreshadowing for Service & Advocacy

Parenting is more than teaching children to read, write, or behave. It is about instilling values that endure beyond the immediate moment, lessons that can shape a life, a community, and ultimately, a legacy. As I reflect on the years raising my children, guiding them through school, extracurricular activities, and the daily challenges of growing up in the Bronx, I realize that every lesson, every conversation, and every consistent action was preparing me for the work I would do beyond my family — for the community I would come to serve.

The routines, the boundaries, the insistence on accountability — these were not just rules; they were training in leadership, responsibility, and long-term thinking. Every morning that I woke my kids, ensured they were fed, prepared for school, and mentally ready for the day, I was practicing skills I would later use to organize community programs, mentor youth, and build a nonprofit. Teaching them about loyalty, honesty, and resilience mirrored the larger lessons needed for any community to thrive.

Raising children in a complex environment taught me that structure is everything. Without routines, guidance, and consistent expectations, even the most capable young people can falter. It became clear to me that community work operates on the same principle: programs must be intentional, repeatable, and sustainable. Mentorship initiatives, youth workshops, and after-school programs are most effective when they have clear rules, trained facilitators, and measurable outcomes — just like parenting requires planning, patience, and follow-through.

Parenting also reinforced the idea of extended family and community as safety nets. I saw the ways that children could flourish when adults around them provided guidance, resources, and support. This lesson shaped my vision for I Am My Community Inc, where the goal was not merely to intervene in crises but to create systems that empower youth, teach accountability, and foster a sense of belonging. Each child's success, each life positively influenced, became a testament to the power of structure, mentorship, and intentional guidance.

Foreshadowing the next chapter, it becomes evident that the skills and principles honed in the home — patience, observation, discipline, and consistent teaching — naturally transitioned into community leadership. The experiences of guiding children, setting boundaries, and nurturing growth became the blueprint for building programs that could operate at scale, impact generations, and create sustainable change. It was no longer enough to survive or even to thrive personally; I understood that my influence could extend far beyond my immediate family, shaping neighborhoods, opportunities, and futures for those who had no one else to guide them.

This chapter closes with the understanding that parenting and community service are inseparable in purpose. Every small act of guidance at home mirrors the work of advocacy in the community. Every lesson imparted to a child — about responsibility, resilience, or loyalty — reflects the principles needed to uplift and strengthen the broader society. The reflections here set the stage for Chapter 6, where service and advocacy become central, transforming lived experience into structured programs, mentorship, and meaningful impact across the Bronx and beyond.

Chapter 6, Part 1 — Launching I Am My Community Inc

The decision to start I Am My Community Inc did not come overnight. It was the culmination of decades of experience — the streets, the classrooms, the studios, the challenges, and the triumphs — all converging into a single purpose: to give back, to guide, and to create opportunities where none existed. I had seen what happened when youth went without guidance: potential squandered, lives cut short, dreams deferred. I knew that a single conversation, a single intervention, could redirect a trajectory that otherwise might have ended in tragedy.

Starting the nonprofit required a combination of vision, planning, and relentless action. I wanted more than an organization that merely existed; I wanted one that worked, adapted, and empowered. The first step was understanding the community's needs. I walked the streets, visited local schools, and spoke with parents, teachers, and youth leaders. Every conversation confirmed what I already knew in my heart: young people needed mentorship, structure, and exposure to positive role models and resources.

The first programs were simple but intentional. We held weekly mentorship circles, giving youth a safe space to talk about challenges, aspirations, and fears. I invited artists, entrepreneurs, and community leaders to share their experiences, demonstrating that success and integrity were achievable. Sports leagues became a platform for teamwork, discipline, and leadership, while food pantries ensured that children had their most basic needs met. Every initiative reinforced a principle I had learned early: opportunity is only as powerful as the structure that supports it.

Building the organization also required understanding the mechanics of sustainability. Volunteers had to be trained, protocols had to be established, and outcomes had to be measurable. I implemented systems for tracking participation, engagement, and progress, ensuring that every program could operate independently yet remain effective. I wanted I Am My Community Inc to endure — to thrive long after my immediate presence, and to touch generations of youth who might never meet me in person.

The work also brought lessons in humility and collaboration. I quickly learned that change does not happen in isolation. Partnerships with schools, local businesses, city agencies, and other nonprofits were essential. Each relationship required negotiation, patience, and trust. I realized that being a leader meant aligning resources, people, and vision — ensuring that everyone involved shared a commitment to integrity, accountability, and empowerment.

Launching I Am My Community Inc was not without challenges. Funding was scarce, skepticism was high, and bureaucratic obstacles were constant. Yet, the energy of the youth, the gratitude of parents, and the small wins in the community reinforced the mission. I understood that impact is cumulative, and that even the smallest intervention — a conversation, a workshop, a mentorship moment — could ripple outward to create profound change.

This part of the story closes with the awareness that service is both a responsibility and a privilege. I Am My Community Inc became the physical manifestation of everything I had learned: the importance of structure, mentorship, loyalty, resilience, and strategic thinking. It was the culmination of street wisdom, life experience, and the desire to ensure that the next generation would have opportunities I wished I had at their age.

Chapter 6, Part 2 — Expanding Programs and Community Impact

Once I Am My Community Inc was established, the next step was to scale its reach while maintaining quality and intention. Starting with a handful of programs and a few committed volunteers, I realized quickly that the youth, families, and neighborhoods needed more than temporary interventions — they needed continuity, structure, and access to resources that could change the trajectory of their lives.

The first expansion involved after-school programs. These were designed to give children and teens a safe space to study, explore creative outlets, and build skills beyond the classroom. I brought in mentors from music, art, sports, and entrepreneurship, each trained to not only teach but also model integrity, discipline, and resilience. Every session reinforced principles I had learned firsthand: teamwork, respect, and the consequences of choices.

Sports programs became a cornerstone of community engagement. Beyond the obvious health and fitness benefits, leagues and tournaments were microcosms of life lessons. Players learned strategy, accountability, and how to navigate competition while respecting rules and authority. Wins and losses became teaching moments; discipline on the field translated into self-discipline off the field.

Food security programs followed, addressing a fundamental barrier to success: hunger. I implemented weekly food pantries and meal distributions that served hundreds of families. Each event reinforced community bonds and highlighted the importance of giving and receiving help with

dignity. The youth learned that support is a two-way street —
that helping others is as important as being helped.

I also developed mentorship pipelines to ensure long-term
impact. Older youth who had benefited from the programs
were invited to mentor younger participants, creating a culture
of peer leadership and responsibility. This structure allowed
lessons to be reinforced and scaled, building a network of
leaders within the community who understood firsthand the
challenges and opportunities their peers faced.

Partnerships with schools, local businesses, and city
agencies were crucial. These collaborations provided
resources, venues, and visibility, while also teaching the
youth about professionalism, networking, and accountability.
By connecting the programs to the broader infrastructure of
the city, I ensured that impact could be measurable,
sustainable, and replicable.

Throughout this expansion, one principle remained at the
center: all programming must empower youth to see
themselves as capable, resilient, and worthy of opportunity.
Every workshop, every mentorship session, and every event
was designed with this goal in mind. The focus was never on
temporary entertainment or quick fixes — it was about
building character, confidence, and competence.

Chapter 6, Part 2 ends with the understanding that service and advocacy are ongoing processes, requiring adaptation, patience, and relentless commitment. The programs were growing, the community was responding, and I was learning alongside every participant. The work was demanding, but the rewards — seeing a child succeed, witnessing a teen find their voice, knowing a family's basic needs were met — were immeasurable.

Chapter 6, Part 3 — Developing Independent Systems

I quickly realized that passion alone was not enough. Energy and good intentions could spark change, but lasting transformation required systems that could survive without me standing over every detail. I began designing every program with intention: every mentorship circle, every after-school activity, every sports league needed structure, rules, and purpose that could outlast a single person's presence.

Volunteers were trained not just to fill roles, but to understand the why behind every action. They learned to observe, guide, and correct without breaking the spirit of the youth. Each protocol, each schedule, and every procedure was built to encourage independence, responsibility, and accountability — not just for the volunteers, but for the participants themselves.

I watched as older kids who had been part of the programs for years began to step into mentorship roles. They carried the lessons forward, not because they were told to, but because they internalized the principles. A boy who had once struggled to attend class began guiding younger students on homework and etiquette. A young woman who had lacked confidence now led art workshops, encouraging her peers to express themselves. The systems allowed their growth to multiply, creating leaders who could inspire without my constant intervention.

Every activity was a carefully orchestrated lesson. Sports became more than competition; they were laboratories for discipline, teamwork, and trust. Workshops were more than instruction; they were arenas where creativity and problem-solving flourished. Even something as simple as a weekly circle of conversation was carefully planned to teach listening, expression, and empathy, with opportunities to practice negotiation, resolve conflicts, and celebrate achievements.

Building these systems was a lesson in patience. Things did not always run smoothly. Mistakes were inevitable, from volunteers forgetting steps to kids testing boundaries. But every setback was an opportunity to refine the process, to reinforce values, and to teach resilience. Slowly, the organization became a living ecosystem, one that could adapt, grow, and thrive, independent of a single person's presence.

Through it all, I learned that leadership is not about doing everything yourself. It is about creating frameworks where others can thrive, where trust and discipline are embedded in the structure, and where impact can expand far beyond a single moment or interaction. I began to see the organization not as mine alone, but as a vessel for the community — capable of empowering youth, inspiring volunteers, and changing neighborhoods.

By the end of this stage, the programs had taken on a life of their own. I could step back slightly and watch the youth succeed, the volunteers guide, and the systems hold. The streets, the mentors, and the lessons of my past had converged into something tangible, scalable, and transformative, something that promised to endure and shape lives for years to come.

Chapter 6, Part 4 — Community Leadership & Long-Term Impact

Leadership is not defined by the size of a crowd or the title on a door; it is defined by the ripples of change that spread from one act of purpose to the lives of many. As the programs of I Am My Community Inc grew, I began to see the subtle ways in which influence shaped behavior, created opportunities, and instilled confidence in those who had long been overlooked.

Walking through the streets, I could feel the impact of what we had built. Kids who once roamed corners aimlessly were now mentoring younger peers, teaching them what I had spent years teaching my own children: responsibility, respect, and foresight. The same youth who had once avoided school were now leaders in after-school workshops, guiding creative projects, and organizing sports leagues. I watched as community ownership blossomed, and for the first time, I realized that the organization was bigger than me.

With each passing year, the network of volunteers and mentors grew stronger. Adults who had once doubted the potential of our programs began to participate actively, share resources, and contribute ideas, reinforcing the principles I had built into the system. Parents expressed gratitude, neighbors began to collaborate, and schools acknowledged the value of having a consistent, structured presence for students outside of the classroom. The change was subtle, gradual, and yet undeniable — a community learning to sustain itself through trust, accountability, and shared purpose.

I also recognized the importance of celebrating achievements, no matter how small. Graduation ceremonies, award nights, and public showcases became moments to honor effort, dedication, and growth. These celebrations were more than recognition; they were evidence that the systems we built could nurture excellence, resilience, and pride. A young man who had struggled with discipline now stood in front of his peers, giving a speech about his journey and the lessons he learned from mentoring programs. A young woman who had once lacked confidence now led a workshop, her voice steady and empowered, inspiring others to follow her example.

Through this work, I began to understand that leadership is not about directing others constantly; it is about equipping people with tools, guidance, and confidence to lead themselves. The youth became teachers, the volunteers became strategists, and the community became a living, evolving ecosystem. The programs no longer required my constant presence to function because we had built a culture of responsibility, initiative, and collaboration.

By the end of this phase, I could reflect on the magnitude of what had been accomplished: a community empowered, youth inspired, and structures designed to last. I had taken lessons from my past — the streets, the mentors, the failures, and the triumphs — and turned them into a blueprint for sustainable impact. Leadership, I realized, is not measured in titles or recognition, but in the enduring strength, confidence, and vision of those you serve.

Chapter 6, Part 5 — Forward Vision & Legacy

Even as programs thrived and youth found purpose, I knew that true leadership and service were about foresight — about building for the future, not just reacting to the present. I began to think not only about the children in the room today, but about those who would walk through our doors in ten, twenty, or thirty years. The work had to be sustainable, scalable, and adaptable, capable of standing the test of time.

I focused on developing future leaders from within the community. Older youth, who had grown under our guidance, were invited to mentor and train the next generation. They were not just following instructions; they were learning to think strategically, solve problems, and inspire others. This approach created a ripple effect: those who had once needed guidance were now providing it, ensuring continuity and longevity of the mission.

Legacy meant embedding values deeply. Every decision, every program design, and every community partnership was rooted in principles that I had learned the hard way: integrity, loyalty, accountability, and foresight. I wanted every participant, volunteer, and partner to internalize these values, so that they could carry them forward into their families, workplaces, and neighborhoods. The goal was not temporary success — it was lasting transformation.

Part of building this legacy was documenting, systematizing, and sharing what worked. Training manuals, volunteer handbooks, and structured program outlines became essential. These resources allowed anyone stepping into the organization to understand, adopt, and enhance the programs without relying solely on my presence. The organization became greater than any single person, a living entity designed to empower the community for generations.

At the same time, I cultivated a vision for advocacy beyond programming. I engaged with local schools, city agencies, and other nonprofits, advocating for policies and initiatives that aligned with the lessons learned on the streets. I knew that lasting change required systemic influence, not just individual mentorship. By creating partnerships and networks, I ensured that the voices of youth and community members were heard, and that opportunities for growth were expanded far beyond our immediate reach.

Forward vision also meant looking inward, reflecting on what legacy I wanted to leave as a human being. I wanted my children and grandchildren, my community, and the youth I served to know that commitment, integrity, and love for others were the markers of a meaningful life. Every story shared, every program implemented, and every life touched became part of a continuum — a testament to what could be achieved when one chooses to serve with purpose.

As I stood at the threshold of this chapter, I understood that legacy was not a single achievement or accolade. It was the lives improved, the lessons taught, and the systems built to empower generations. It was about creating a foundation strong enough that even when I was gone, the work would continue, thriving in the hands of those inspired to carry it forward.

Chapter 7, Part 1 — The Blackout and the Streets

2003.   The city was tense. News reports warned of a blackout later that day, and I was living in the projects on 170th and Washington Avenue. My youngest daughter had just been born, and every decision I made had to account for her safety and well-being. Even small choices felt monumental.

That afternoon, my baby mother went uptown to visit a friend. She left her phone behind, and I knew I had no other way to contact her. I had to get to her before the darkness fell, before the streets became unpredictable. Walking through the block, I noticed how quiet the city felt — almost like it was holding its breath, anticipating the chaos to come. The hum of the streets, the scent of food from corner vendors, the occasional shout from a passing car — it all seemed amplified in that looming darkness.

I was only five minutes uptown when a police car pulled up behind me, sirens silent but lights flashing faintly. They approached quickly and instructed me to get in. My mind raced. Why me? Why now? I had no outstanding reason to be stopped, no immediate threat, nothing on record that should have drawn attention.

Once inside the precinct, I was processed and placed in a cell. The officers left to handle the emergency elsewhere. Minutes passed like hours. I kept my composure, but the uncertainty gnawed at me. Who knew why I was here? What charges would they claim? Then a female officer returned and, with a tremor in her voice, revealed what had me frozen in disbelief: I was being held for murder.

I remember standing there, trying to make sense of it. My mind replayed every detail: the apartment, the streets, the people I had passed. Nothing connected. No lineups, no witnesses, no court date — just a name and a charge. Fear and disbelief collided with the instinct to protect myself and my daughter. My thoughts raced: How could this happen? How could a system so massive, so seemingly meticulous, allow for this kind of error?

The first hours on Rikers Island were surreal. The weight of incarceration, even for something I did not commit, was suffocating. I observed the men around me — some hardened by years, others like me, shocked and unsure. It was a lesson in human behavior under pressure: some showed solidarity, some avoided attention, and some tested the limits of control. I learned quickly that survival required patience, observation, and restraint.

Even in the chaos, my thoughts never left my daughter. Every echo of the clanging cell doors reminded me of the fragility of life and freedom. I swore to myself that no matter what came next, I would emerge stronger, wiser, and ready to fight for justice with clarity, not anger.

The blackout loomed outside, but inside those walls, time moved differently. Minutes stretched into hours, and hours into days. Each moment was a test — a test of endurance, self-control, and mental fortitude. I realized that true strength is measured not by brute force, but by the ability to maintain integrity under impossible circumstances.

That night, the city went dark, and the streets I knew so well became a shadowed landscape of uncertainty. Yet inside me, a different kind of light burned: a determination that no matter how unjust or overwhelming the system appeared, I would navigate it, survive it, and turn the experience into lessons that could guide others.

By dawn, the first part of this chapter in my life had passed — a crucible that tested my instincts, my judgment, and my resilience. It was only the beginning of a series of events that would shape my understanding of justice, responsibility, and leadership in ways that I would carry for the rest of my life.

Chapter 7, Part 2 — The Rikers Experience

Rikers Island. Just saying the name sent chills through me, but now I was inside, and there was no escaping the reality. The gates, the razor wire, the distant shouts — everything felt designed to strip you of control, to remind you of the world you had just entered. I wasn't there for something I had done, yet the weight of the environment pressed down on me as though I had committed the gravest crimes imaginable.

The first day was an orientation in survival. Every man in the cellhouse was sizing you up, and every glance carried unspoken rules. The stories I had heard about Rikers didn't capture the rhythm of fear, vigilance, and careful observation that governed every second. You learned quickly: every word you spoke, every movement you made, could determine whether you became invisible or a target.

I observed my surroundings with acute attention. Men who appeared calm were often the most dangerous; those who shouted the loudest were often the most vulnerable. The dynamic was subtle, almost invisible to the untrained eye.

Here, the ability to read a room, gauge intent, and act deliberately wasn't optional — it was survival.

I was escorted to a cell shared with two others. Silence was the currency at first; conversation came slowly, measured, until trust began to form. Over time, I realized that the people who were able to maintain dignity under pressure were also the ones who endured, the ones who carried themselves with a quiet authority that needed no recognition. I studied them, learning not just how to survive physically, but how to navigate the psychology of confinement.

Daily routines became both a lifeline and a lesson. The monotony of meals, the regimented movements, the endless roll calls — each repetition offered a chance to observe patterns, anticipate outcomes, and exercise self-discipline. In this rigid world, I found pockets of control where I could preserve my identity, where my thoughts and intentions remained my own.

I also witnessed the consequences of choices firsthand. Some men were consumed by anger, others by despair, and some by manipulation of those around them. In every interaction, there was a lesson: loyalty, honesty, and integrity were often more valuable than brute strength. These were the same principles I had tried to instill in my community outside, now mirrored in the microcosm of incarceration.

Evenings brought reflection. The city outside was dark, disconnected from me, and I felt the fragility of freedom in ways I never had before. Yet, amid the fear and uncertainty, I discovered resilience. Every day on Rikers became a mirror: if I could maintain my composure, my principles, and my sense of purpose here, I could navigate any challenge outside those walls.

I began to write in my mind — stories, lessons, plans, visions of how to turn this ordeal into wisdom. I thought about the youth I had worked with, the future programs, the families depending on me. Every experience on Rikers became fuel, a lesson in strategy, patience, and long-term thinking.

By the end of my time in that cellhouse, I realized Rikers Island was not just a place of punishment — it was a crucible, refining the way I thought about justice, leadership, and accountability. It was shaping me not into someone hardened by fear, but into someone capable of transforming experience into guidance, and pain into purpose.

Chapter 7, Part 3 — The Grand Jury and Legal Challenges

After my time on Rikers Island, I was brought before the grand jury. Walking into that courtroom, I felt the weight of every accusation, every assumption, and every expectation bearing down on me. It wasn't just about the law — it was about how the system viewed someone like me: a young Black man from the Bronx, familiar with the streets, and now caught in a machinery that seemed indifferent to truth.

The grand jury process was unlike anything I had ever experienced. Questions were asked that assumed guilt rather than explored fact. I answered honestly, and repeatedly, clarifying that I had never been in a lineup, never participated in any prior investigation, and never had a chance to defend myself in the ways others could take for granted. Every answer was met with skepticism or disbelief. I could feel the tension in the room, the impatience, the subtle judgment.

But I refused to let frustration cloud my resolve. Every response, every pause, every tone of my voice was a statement of integrity. I realized that defending myself wasn't just about this case; it was about standing for what was right in the midst of injustice. It was about showing the next generation that truth, courage, and composure mattered more than intimidation, assumption, or force.

The grand jury seemed endless. Hours stretched into days. I listened as attorneys debated, as witnesses spoke, as prosecutors attempted to weave a narrative I did not recognize. And yet, I learned to navigate this theater with calm observation, strategic answers, and mental clarity. My training in the streets, my experience on Rikers, and the discipline I had built into my life all converged in those moments.

One question from the foreman cut through the tension: "Have you ever been in a lineup or photo array?" My answer was simple: "No." It was a small answer, but it carried the weight of truth against presumption. The room seemed to pause; the foreman's inquiry was not just procedural — it was a test of character, and I held my ground.

Through this ordeal, I realized that the law is not always the same as justice. The grand jury was a reminder that systems are imperfect, that decisions are made in the shadow of bias and human error. But I also saw that the way one carries themselves in the face of systemic pressure can define the outcome as much as the law itself.

By the time the process concluded, I had learned invaluable lessons about resilience, strategic thinking, and the power of truth. I walked out with more than relief; I walked out with clarity. Every challenge, every questioning, every unjust assumption was a lesson in how to navigate authority, influence outcomes, and maintain integrity under pressure.

That experience became a foundation for my later work in leadership and advocacy. I understood that real change required not only courage but also a deep understanding of how systems operate, and how to use knowledge, observation, and strategy to protect those who cannot protect themselves.

Chapter 7, Part 4 — Mentorship & Community Leadership

Emerging from the challenges of Rikers and the grand jury, I realized that personal survival was not enough. The streets, the system, and the neighborhoods I had grown up in demanded more than resilience — they demanded action, guidance, and leadership. I couldn't just survive for myself; I needed to create pathways for others to thrive where too many had stumbled.

That realization sparked the foundation of mentorship as a central part of my life. I knew firsthand how much a single conversation, a guiding hand, or an example of discipline could change a young person's trajectory. It was not about telling them what to do, but showing them through experience, honesty, and presence.

I began small. I would walk through the neighborhoods, noticing youth loitering, frustrated, or misdirected. I would approach them, not with judgment, but with questions: "What are your goals? What do you want to see in your life? Who believes in you?" Often, these questions were the first time anyone had asked them directly.

I learned that mentorship required trust, and trust wasn't given lightly. Many kids had been let down by adults in the past.

They were wary, guarded, sometimes even hostile. So I had to prove my authenticity through consistency, patience, and presence. I attended basketball games, school events, and block parties, showing up when others would not. Every small interaction reinforced the principle that mentorship was built on credibility and reliability.

In these interactions, I discovered the transformative power of storytelling as a teaching tool. I shared my own experiences — the arrests, the jail time, the mistakes — not to glorify them, but to illustrate the consequences of choices and the value of learning from every experience. When a young person heard that someone who had been in the same neighborhoods, faced similar dangers, and survived was willing to invest time in them, they listened differently.

Leadership also meant creating structures to scale the impact. It wasn't enough to mentor a handful of youth; I wanted the programs to reach the next generation and the next, long after I was no longer physically present. I began developing formal programs, recruiting volunteers, and establishing protocols that ensured mentorship could operate effectively at every level.

Each mentor I trained became a multiplier. They carried the lessons forward, guiding other youth with the same principles of honesty, integrity, and accountability. I realized that true leadership was about leaving a legacy of empowerment — not just influence through presence, but through systems that could grow and thrive independently.

Through these efforts, I also learned about the delicate balance between guidance and autonomy. Young people needed direction, but they also needed to make their own decisions, succeed on their own terms, and fail safely when necessary. Part of mentorship was watching from the sidelines, ready to intervene when needed, but allowing room for growth, experimentation, and personal responsibility.

By the end of this phase of my work, mentorship had become more than a program — it was a philosophy, a way of life. It shaped not only the youth I guided but also the adults I worked with, creating a community of accountability, support, and shared vision. Each success reinforced the truth I had learned on the streets and in the courts: invest in people, and they will invest in the world around them.

Chapter 7, Part 5 — Building Systems That Last

It became clear that mentorship alone wasn't enough. Showing up, speaking to youth, or even organizing events could help temporarily, but if there were no structures to sustain the work, the impact would fade the moment I wasn't present. I needed to design systems that could operate independently, that could teach, guide, and uplift even without my daily supervision.

I started by mapping out every aspect of our programs. After-school activities, community workshops, youth mentoring sessions — each required clear protocols, training guides, and accountability mechanisms. I worked closely with volunteers, taking the time to teach not just the 'how' but the 'why'. Every activity had a purpose: to instill responsibility, resilience, and opportunity.

We developed tracking mechanisms to monitor progress. Attendance, engagement, skill development — each metric was carefully recorded and analyzed. If a program wasn't working, we adapted it. If a volunteer struggled, we provided additional support. I realized that systems were not static; they had to evolve with the needs of the community and the challenges of the moment.

Building these systems taught me the importance of sustainability. It was no longer about my personal energy or charisma — it was about creating frameworks that would endure beyond any single person. Volunteers were trained to become leaders in their own right, able to mentor, manage, and innovate independently. Youth participants could eventually become mentors themselves, passing on lessons to the next generation.

One of the most powerful lessons I learned in this process was about leverage. With a single, well-structured system, a small team could reach dozens, hundreds, or even thousands of young people. Impact multiplied exponentially. A program that seemed modest at first could, with the right design, influence entire neighborhoods.

In the process of building systems, I also confronted my own limitations. I realized I could not be everywhere, solve every problem, or personally mentor every child in need. The solution was architecture over presence — creating processes that did the work even when I wasn't physically there. This mindset reshaped how I approached leadership: from reactive to proactive, from temporary to permanent.

By the end of this phase, I saw the results. Programs ran smoothly, youth engagement improved, and the community began to internalize the lessons we were teaching. Volunteers and youth alike felt empowered because they were active participants in the design and execution. The systems were no longer just tools; they had become a living, evolving reflection of the values we believed in: integrity, loyalty, and empowerment.

Building systems was more than leadership; it was legacy creation. Each program, each protocol, each mentor trained was a seed planted for the future. The lessons learned here — patience, foresight, adaptability — became the blueprint for all my future advocacy work. It was proof that true leadership is measured not just in deeds but in the structures you leave behind that can continue to do good long after your own work is done.

Chapter 7, Part 6 — Advocacy and Outreach

Once the systems were in place, I realized that the work needed to extend beyond the walls of our programs. Mentorship and structured activities were powerful, but real change required engagement with the broader community, the city, and even local policymakers. Advocacy became the bridge between individual empowerment and systemic transformation.

I started attending community board meetings, city council forums, and public hearings. Every time I spoke, I drew from my own experiences — the streets, the hardships, the arrests, the lessons learned. My goal was clear: to ensure that the youth in our neighborhoods had voices, opportunities, and support systems that I had once lacked.

Outreach was not just about visibility; it was about creating partnerships. I reached out to local schools, religious institutions, and businesses, demonstrating how they could play a role in mentorship, provide resources, and offer safe spaces for youth. I emphasized the importance of collaboration over competition, showing that the community itself could be a network of support rather than a collection of isolated efforts.

One of the most important elements of advocacy was storytelling as truth-telling. I shared the realities of street life, the pitfalls that had ensnared so many, and the successes of those who had been guided toward better choices. These stories were powerful tools, not to glorify struggle but to illustrate consequences, resilience, and the possibility of transformation.

I also began creating programs specifically for parents and guardians, teaching them how to engage with their children, reinforce positive behaviors, and navigate systems that often seemed indifferent to their struggles. Many adults had experienced the streets themselves, and I had to meet them where they were — with empathy, patience, and practical guidance.

Media and technology became a part of our outreach strategy. Social media, community newsletters, and local radio allowed us to broadcast messages of hope, awareness, and opportunity. I made sure that the message was consistent: the community could take responsibility for its youth, empower them with resources, and change the trajectory of entire neighborhoods.

Advocacy also meant pushing for policy changes. I met with council members, spoke with nonprofit coalitions, and participated in panels about youth crime prevention, education equity, and safe recreational spaces. Every conversation was a chance to translate street knowledge into actionable policy, showing that solutions needed to be informed by those closest to the problem.

Through outreach and advocacy, I learned a profound truth: leadership is not about authority; it's about influence and responsibility. The more people I could inspire, teach, and mobilize, the more enduring our impact became. Each small victory — a child entering college, a parent reconnecting with their child, a community event that brought neighbors together — was proof that systemic change begins with committed, persistent action.

By the end of this phase, I understood that empowerment was multi-layered: it wasn't enough to guide individuals; the structures, policies, and culture of the community itself had to evolve. This work taught me that lasting change requires vision, strategy, and relentless execution — qualities that would carry me forward into the final stages of my leadership and into the legacy I hoped to leave.

Chapter 7, Part 7 — Forward Vision & Legacy

As the systems, programs, and advocacy efforts matured, I began to think beyond the immediate impact. Leadership, I realized, was not just measured by today's successes, but by the enduring structures and values left behind for future generations. Forward vision meant planning for decades, not months, and ensuring that the work would continue without me at the center.

I envisioned a community where mentorship was a standard, not an exception. Where youth had access to opportunities, guidance, and safe spaces — not because of luck or chance, but because the infrastructure of care, education, and empowerment was embedded into the neighborhood itself. Every program, every protocol, every volunteer trained was a building block toward that vision.

Legacy, I understood, was more than personal accolades or recognition. It was about shaping culture and expectation, showing young people that integrity, resilience, and responsibility could create pathways to success, even in the most challenging environments. I worked to ensure that the principles I valued — loyalty, honesty, diligence, and service — were woven into every part of our operations, from mentorship sessions to citywide initiatives.

I also reflected on the families in the community. Too often, parents were overlooked, struggling silently. I emphasized programs that engaged the entire household, teaching parents how to guide, protect, and support their children. The goal was holistic change: empowering youth while strengthening the foundations of the families who raised them.

Forward vision also meant preparing for scale. I considered how programs could expand across neighborhoods and boroughs, how partnerships could multiply our impact, and how lessons learned locally could influence citywide policy. Every strategy was built with sustainability in mind — a network of leaders, mentors, and community members capable of carrying the mission forward.

I thought about the next generation — my children, my grandchildren, and every child who walked through our programs. I imagined a world where they would not have to navigate the streets alone, where they would inherit not chaos, but guidance, opportunity, and a community invested in their success. That vision became the compass for every decision, every plan, and every new initiative.

By the time this chapter of my life was concluding, I realized that true leadership is timeless. It transcends individual action and becomes a living framework for others to follow. Legacy is not merely remembered — it is felt, lived, and perpetuated by those who inherit the structures, lessons, and principles laid down before them.

And so, as I looked ahead, I committed to ensure that my work, my lessons, and my values would continue to shape lives long after I was gone, creating a cycle of empowerment and hope that could endure for generations to come.

SECTION C — CONTINUITY & FUTURE

HUSTLE & GRIND MOVERS & SHAKERS NETWORK
PRESENTS

2023 DROP YO SELFIE
HIP HOP LEGENDARY AWARD

TO:

THE LORD K-BORN

Drop Yo Selfie

Time carried forward. This image reflects endurance shaped into wisdom.

CERTIFICATE
OF LEADERSHIP
Darney "K-Born Rivers
FOR YOUR OUTSTANDING SERVICE TO THE COMMUNITY & SOCIETY
COMRADE DON CURTIS
FOUNDER/PRESIDENT
UBC
2024
TONIA VAIL
DIRECTOR OF
OPERATIONS

Responsibility passed. What we protect today becomes tomorrow's inheritance.

PEACE
19 71
MAKERS

Memory as guide. The future learns from what was
preserved.

HAYMAKER
The Assembly
State of New York
Proclamation

Continuance. Not an ending, but a handoff.

Chapter 8 — Answers and Solutions

Part 1: Personal Accountability

Accountability is one of the hardest lessons a person can truly internalize. It's easy to point fingers, blame circumstances, or rationalize mistakes, but life does not bend to excuses. The moment we take ownership of our actions, choices, and their consequences, we begin to unlock power — the kind that changes our trajectory, shapes relationships, and builds respect.

I learned accountability in the streets long before I saw it in classrooms or boardrooms. Every choice I made — good or bad — rippled outward, affecting friends, family, and the community. One wrong decision could lead to a night in jail; one right choice could save a life. Accountability is not reactive; it's proactive. It requires clarity about who you are, what you want, and how your actions affect those around you.

I teach the youth I mentor about the 3 C's of Accountability:

- Clarity: Understand your role in every situation. Know the difference between actions within your control and circumstances outside it. Recognize patterns in behavior that either lift you or weigh you down.

- Commitment: Once you acknowledge responsibility, commit to change. The promise to yourself is more important than anyone else's approval. Stay consistent. Show up every day, even when it's uncomfortable.

- Consequences: Accept the outcomes — rewards or penalties. Learning to sit with the result of your actions, without deflection or blame, is the core of growth. Consequences are lessons dressed in reality.

I tell the youth: if you cheat, lie, or fail to honor your word, the world will remember before you do. But if you stand by your word, even when nobody is watching, you create a foundation of trust that will carry you further than any street hustle, any degree, or any paycheck. A person breaking their word can lose more than money; it can cost friendships, opportunities, or even safety. Conversely, a person keeping their word can unlock doors that seem impossible to open.

Accountability is also about self-reflection. Daily, I look at my actions, the words I use, and the promises I make. I ask myself: Did I honor my values today? Did I act in a way that aligns with the man I want my children and grandchildren to emulate? If not, I adjust immediately. This habit became a cornerstone of my growth — in life, in leadership, and in community service.

Even at moments when I faced legal trouble or personal loss, holding myself accountable allowed me to survive, learn, and transform. It's a discipline that builds resilience and trustworthiness, qualities that are rarer than talent, more valuable than gold, and more enduring than fame.

Practical Tip: Write down your daily choices and reflect on how each action impacts others. Use it as a roadmap for improvement, no matter how small the steps may seem.

Hotline Resource: If you need guidance on accountability, life direction, or mental health support, call 1-800-662-4357 (SAMHSA). Professionals are there to guide you without judgment — a reminder that accountability starts with recognizing when help is necessary.

Chapter 8 — Answers and Solutions

Part 2: Community Strategies

No individual can thrive in isolation, and no neighborhood can transform without collective effort. Over the years, I've realized that creating meaningful change requires intentional strategies, not random acts of goodwill. Communities need structures, plans, and systems that allow residents to lift each other up, protect each other, and sustain progress over time.

Experts identify six strategies of community change:

1. Mass Mobilization – Rallying people toward a shared goal. It's the power of thousands acting with a single purpose, whether it's a neighborhood cleanup, a food drive, or a campaign to create safer streets. In the Bronx, we organized community events where hundreds of neighbors came together to reclaim public spaces and establish pride in the block. The energy from mass mobilization is contagious; it creates momentum that cannot be ignored.

2. Social Action – Taking deliberate steps to address injustices and inequities. This could mean organizing petitions, hosting educational forums, or confronting a problem head-on. Social action is about visibility and accountability, demonstrating that residents will not remain silent in the face of harm or neglect.

3. Citizen Participation – Everyone must have a voice. Encouraging residents to join community boards, attend city council meetings, or volunteer in youth programs ensures that decisions reflect lived experience. It is remarkable how often the people closest to a problem have the best solutions; the trick is getting them to speak up and act.

4. Public Advocacy – Engaging with policymakers, agencies, and local leaders to influence decisions. Over my years with I Am My Community Inc, I've learned that a single letter, phone call, or personal visit can create ripples that change entire systems. Advocacy is not confrontation; it's presenting facts, lived experience, and actionable solutions in a way that leaders cannot ignore.

5. Popular Education – Knowledge is power. Sharing what you know empowers others to take action. We created workshops, mentorship programs, and community seminars that teach youth about safety, opportunity, and leadership. Educated residents become agents of change, passing on skills, awareness, and insight to the next generation.

6. Local Services Development – Building programs that address real needs: food pantries, after-school activities, mental health workshops, and skill-building courses. These services create tangible impact while teaching accountability, responsibility, and community values.

I have seen firsthand how these strategies intersect. A youth mentorship program might involve education, citizen participation, and local services simultaneously. When residents feel empowered to take ownership of their neighborhood, change becomes self-sustaining.

Actionable Advice: If you want to change your community, start small. Attend a local meeting, organize a block cleanup, or mentor a child. Momentum grows from consistent effort, and your actions will inspire others to join.

Hotline/Resource: For guidance on community organizing or volunteer opportunities, call 1-866-827-3747 (NeighborWorks America). They provide support and structure for residents looking to build safer, stronger communities.

Chapter 8 — Answers and Solutions

Part 3: Education & Opportunity

Education is the foundation of possibility. I have always believed that knowledge is power, and access to education is a lifeline for communities like mine. The streets teach lessons about survival, loyalty, and resourcefulness, but formal education equips a person to navigate systems, claim opportunity, and break cycles of hardship.

From a young age, I saw the value of learning. While my peers were hustling or getting lost in distractions, I found ways to expand my mind and sharpen my skills. In my nonprofit work with I Am My Community Inc, I emphasize to youth and parents that the resources exist — often free — if we choose to take advantage of them. GED classes, OSHA 40-hour courses, and CDL licenses are not just credentials; they are tools that open doors, shift mindsets, and give young people options beyond the block.

I tell youth: "Education can be the coolest thing on the block." It starts with framing it as a choice, a challenge, and a personal victory. When a young person passes a GED test or earns a certification, it is celebrated like a championship. This recognition builds confidence, fosters pride, and reinforces the message that success is possible.

Summer youth jobs are another powerful avenue. By engaging in structured work, kids earn money, build experience, and see a world outside the immediate pressures of their neighborhood. I've watched young people transform after just one summer of mentorship, work, and exposure to professional standards. It's proof that opportunity changes behavior and perspective.

Parents play a vital role. Signing kids up for programs, encouraging them to attend classes, celebrating small wins — these are not optional actions; they are investments in a lifetime of impact. Showing interest and participating in their growth communicates a message stronger than any lecture.

Practical Tip: Take inventory of the resources around you. Many community colleges, technical schools, and online programs offer free or low-cost courses. Sign up, encourage others, and make learning visible and celebrated.

Hotline/Resource: For GED programs and educational guidance, call 1-800-628-0222 (GED Testing Service). For additional career and skill-building programs, check local community centers or colleges.

Education and opportunity are not abstract ideals; they are actionable pathways. The youth of today can leverage these tools to break cycles, elevate families, and reshape neighborhoods. With mentorship, access, and encouragement, knowledge becomes the most powerful currency a young person can earn.

Chapter 8 — Answers and Solutions

Part 4: Advocacy & Policy Change

Change does not happen in isolation. To transform a community, to protect its youth, and to ensure opportunity, we must understand the structures that govern us and actively participate in shaping them. Advocacy and policy change are not just for elected officials; they are tools every resident can wield to make neighborhoods safer, stronger, and more equitable.

I learned early that many people don't know who represents them, which community board governs their building, or even the district they live in. This knowledge is power, and with it comes the responsibility to act. It begins with asking questions, attending local meetings, and making your voice heard.

Advocacy can take many forms:

- Writing letters or emails to your local representatives.

- Attending community board sessions to present issues affecting your block.

- Organizing neighborhood meetings to discuss challenges and solutions.

- Collaborating with nonprofits to lobby for programs, funding, or legislation.

Real advocacy is persistent and informed. It requires research, patience, and the ability to present lived experience as credible evidence. I've walked into meetings and heard skepticism, yet every story, every fact shared, was a testament to the power of being prepared and committed. Change is not instantaneous, but when community members engage collectively, even small actions accumulate into systemic progress.

Policy change is intertwined with awareness. Residents must push for transparency, accountability, and the protection of youth. For example, advocating for after-school programs, safer parks, or youth employment opportunities directly impacts lives. Policies aren't abstract rules; they are instruments that shape everyday experiences. A policy that funds summer youth jobs or GED programs may be the difference between a teen walking toward opportunity or being pulled into crime.

Practical Tip: Identify your elected officials — city council, state assembly, or local boards — and commit to engaging with at least one issue this year. Volunteer, attend hearings, or provide testimony. Every voice counts, and your lived experience matters.

Hotline/Resource: For guidance on civic engagement or local advocacy programs, visit www.nyc.gov or call 311 for local government services.

True leadership is about empowering others to understand and influence the systems around them. Advocacy and policy change are not optional; they are essential for building sustainable, thriving communities. By teaching youth and adults to engage, we create a culture where solutions are pursued collectively, and the next generation grows up knowing that their voice matters.

Chapter 8 — Answers and Solutions

Part 5: Family & Parenting Solutions

Being a parent is one of the most challenging and rewarding roles a person can hold. It is not about being friends; it is about guiding, protecting, and preparing the next generation for life's realities. I've learned that the smallest gestures — saying "I love you," showing up consistently, setting clear boundaries — can shape a child's world far more than grandiose promises ever could.

From the day my first daughter was born, I understood the weight of responsibility. At 17, I was still a child myself, yet I had to step into a role that demanded maturity, discipline, and foresight. Every decision mattered. Every action had ripple effects. I taught my children that respect is reciprocal, that boundaries are necessary, and that love must be demonstrated daily.

Time and communication are at the core of effective parenting. It's not enough to be present physically; parents must engage emotionally and mentally. I structured my days to attend school events, participate in trips, and make myself available to answer questions, solve problems, and instill values. I wanted my children to know that while mistakes happen, there is always a safe space to learn and grow.

Discipline is a cornerstone, but it is more than punishment. It is teaching accountability, helping children understand consequences for choices, and ensuring that the lessons last beyond the moment. By modeling responsible behavior, showing honesty, and maintaining integrity, parents can empower children to navigate life independently.

I also emphasize the importance of professional help when needed. Mental health, counseling, and guidance are not signs of weakness; they are tools for resilience. Families that communicate openly and normalize seeking help foster emotional intelligence, stability, and long-term success.

Practical Advice:

- Establish daily rituals of connection, even brief check-ins.

- Set clear rules and expectations that are consistent.

- Celebrate achievements — big and small — to reinforce growth.

- Demonstrate love openly; children internalize actions, not just words.

Hotline/Resource: For parenting support or family guidance, call 1-800-422-4453 (National Parent Helpline).

Parenting is the foundation of community transformation. By shaping responsible, resilient, and empowered children, we invest in the future of neighborhoods, cities, and generations. Every lesson, every conversation, every moment matters. Family solutions are not temporary fixes; they are the blueprint for generational success.

Chapter 8 — Answers and Solutions

Part 6: Maintaining Hope, Mental Health & Forward Vision

Hope is not passive; it is an active choice, a daily decision to keep moving forward even when circumstances feel insurmountable. I have seen the devastation that lack of guidance, untreated trauma, and unchecked mental health challenges can create in neighborhoods like mine. Too often, communities normalize suffering — the gunfire, the losses, the instability — and fail to recognize that healing is a responsibility we all share.

Mental health is as critical as any other aspect of survival. Many individuals in the Bronx and similar communities carry trauma they barely understand. They adapt by numbing emotions or embracing the chaos around them, but untreated mental illness can lead to despair, risky behaviors, and generational patterns of pain. Recognizing and addressing mental health is an act of courage.

I encourage youth, parents, and community members to view mental health as a resource, not a stigma. Therapy, counseling, and guidance are not privileges; they are lifelines. I've made sure that through I Am My Community Inc, resources and access to professionals are available — because a single conversation or intervention can redirect a life.

Hotline/Resources:

- National Alliance on Mental Illness (NAMI): 1-800-950-6264

- SAMHSA Helpline: 1-800-662-4357

Forward vision means planning for sustainability, impact, and legacy. I've built I Am My Community Inc with systems that continue beyond my direct involvement — mentorship programs, youth initiatives, community workshops — ensuring that lessons, opportunities, and guidance persist across generations. Leadership is not measured by the present alone; it is judged by the structures left for those who come next.

Maintaining hope requires action. I encourage everyone to invest in themselves, seek help when needed, and commit to being a stabilizing force for others. Every effort to educate, mentor, or guide a youth, every initiative to improve a neighborhood, is a direct investment in hope.

Finally, the collective legacy is a culmination of our work, values, and vision. I envision a Bronx and neighborhoods like it where children grow up with opportunity, adults collaborate instead of compete destructively, and communities thrive because people choose accountability, care, and action every day. This vision is alive in every program we run, every life we touch, and every lesson we impart.

Resource & Website: For ongoing community engagement and programs, visit www.iammycommunityinc.com.

Epilogue — Family, Grandchildren, and Legacy

As I sit back and reflect on the life I've lived, I see the threads that connect everything: the streets, the struggles, the victories, the losses, and the lessons. And at the center of it all, standing as the most profound source of joy and purpose, are my grandchildren. Six lives, three boys and three girls, ranging from just two months old to twenty years, each carrying their own energy, curiosity, and promise.

My grandchildren are a mirror of hope. Every time I walk into a room where they are laughing, playing, or asking questions, I see the future I fought for, the lives I hoped to influence, and the cycles I wanted to break. There is no pretense with them — in their eyes, I am not defined by my mistakes, my arrests, or my time in the system. I am grandad, grandp, granddaddy — a constant in their world, someone who shows up, listens, and loves without condition.

During summer breaks, I take them under my wing for the entire season. We fill the days with exploration, adventure, and learning: trips to museums, community events, parks, and local neighborhoods that I know shaped me. We laugh together, and sometimes we get quiet, sharing stories that reveal the complexity of life, the importance of choices, and the resilience of the human spirit. Nights are filled with movies, whispered advice, and conversations that linger long after the lights go out.

Distance has never diminished these bonds. Though my grandchildren live in North Carolina and I reside in the Bronx, our connection is constant. Phone calls, video chats, and letters keep our conversations alive. When they return to visit, it's as if no time has passed at all — their energy fills the house, and I am reminded that legacy is not measured in proximity, but in the love, guidance, and attention we pour into those we cherish.

Watching my grandchildren grow has also reaffirmed a truth I have carried for decades: the importance of building systems that endure beyond our presence. The lessons I teach them, the principles I instill, the values I model — these are all part of a living legacy that they will carry forward, influencing their peers, their communities, and eventually their own children.

My dreams for the family extend beyond moments of laughter and joy. I envision a home large enough to house every child and grandchild, a place where we can gather, celebrate, and continue the cycle of mentorship and guidance. I want every one of them to feel the safety, love, and opportunities I strived to create, so that they can thrive without the obstacles that challenged me.

But legacy is not only about family. It is also about community, service, and the choices we make in shaping the world around us. Every program I built, every youth I mentored, every advocate I trained — these are extensions of the same philosophy that drives me with my grandchildren: invest in people, nurture potential, and leave the world better than you found it.

As I look forward, I see that life is a continuum. The lessons of the past, the work of the present, and the vision for the future are all intertwined. My grandchildren are a daily reminder that what we build today can inspire, protect, and empower generations yet to come. In their eyes, I see hope. In their laughter, I hear purpose. And in their dreams, I recognize the reflection of everything I fought to create — a legacy of resilience, love, and unwavering commitment to people, family, and community.

The story does not end here. It lives on in each child
mentored, every program sustained, and every grandchild
nurtured. The life I have led, the choices I have made, and the
systems I have built — all converge to form a simple truth: we
are the stewards of the future, and it is our responsibility to
leave it better than we found it.

About the Author

Darney K. "K Born" Rivers is a Bronx native whose life story embodies resilience, transformation, and dedication to community. From humble beginnings in the Bronx, he navigated the challenges of urban life, early loss, and legal struggles to emerge as a leader, mentor, and advocate for youth and families.

As the founder of I Am My Community Inc, Darney has created sustainable programs that empower young people, provide resources for families, and cultivate safer, stronger neighborhoods. His work spans mentorship, advocacy, education, and community engagement, reflecting a philosophy that the closest people to a problem often hold the keys to its solution.

Darney is also a celebrated artist, whose hip-hop legacy spans decades. He is known for his landmark track "New Generation", produced by Teddy Riley, which helped define a new era in music. Beyond music, Darney's life experiences — from navigating the streets, incarceration, and personal loss — inform his writing, teaching, and public service.

He has been recognized with numerous awards, proclamations, and community honors, and he continues to work tirelessly to build systems of empowerment, leaving a legacy for future generations.

Through his memoir, Darney shares hard-earned lessons on accountability, leadership, survival, and hope, offering readers a blueprint to navigate life's challenges and create meaningful change in their own communities.

Author's Note

This memoir is not about perfection. It is about evolution, about the mistakes that teach, the hardships that shape, and the redemption that follows. It is about loyalty, resilience, and the courage it takes to stand up even when the world seems determined to keep you down.

I did not write these pages to glorify the past, nor to present myself as someone without flaws. I wrote this book because stories have the power to save lives. To inspire someone, to guide someone, to help someone see that even in the darkest corners, there is a path forward.

Within these chapters, you will find the streets I grew up on, the lessons learned from family, mentors, and mistakes, and the work I have done to transform pain into purpose. You will meet the people who shaped me, the challenges that tested me, and the victories that reminded me of the power of perseverance.

If even one young person reads these pages and chooses a better path, if even one family finds guidance in these stories, then every moment spent writing, reflecting, and remembering has been worth it.

Chapter 2, Part 1 — Elementary Years & Early School Life

School was always a place of discovery for me, but it was also a battlefield of curiosity, social negotiation, and early lessons in consequences. From the first days at Junior High School 22 on 167th Street and Morris Avenue, I quickly realized that every action, even those taken without full understanding, could have serious outcomes.

In the 4th grade, I went with a few friends to a local junior high after school. One of the kids took a watch from a younger student. I didn't run, and in truth, I barely knew most of the other kids involved. But the next morning, police arrived in our classroom, and I was arrested for the first time in my life. I was not afraid, but I felt a profound shame — it was my mother's birthday, a day that should have been filled with celebration and not handcuffs.

When my mother arrived at the precinct around 7 pm after work, she calmly picked me up. One of the officers suggested she should punish me physically, but she simply shook her head and said: "It's my birthday. If I hit him today, I might end up killing him." That moment wasn't just a memory — it was a lesson in restraint, perspective, and the power of parental love, shaping the way I would respond to crises for the rest of my life.

Even at this young age, I was naturally drawn to people, leadership, and social observation. My mother often warned me, "You're too curious. Don't slow me down. Don't distract others. Keep your eyes open, but don't get lost in the crowd." By the time I was five or six, I had a network of friends older than me, mentors in the neighborhood, and a way of speaking with adults that belied my age. I could spend hours talking, learning, and observing — the first glimmers of my later ability to read people, situations, and systems.

School itself was a mix of structure and improvisation. I loved attending the P.A.L. programs, where teachers like Mrs. Puckerin, Mrs. Smalls/Harris, and Mr. Julius ran classrooms not by age but by ability. Those two classrooms became microcosms of the world: students challenged, tested, and supported each other in ways standard schools could never replicate. Discipline was strict but rooted in care — skipping class, fighting, or misbehaving wasn't just noted; consequences followed swiftly, often in partnership with parents. These experiences ingrained responsibility, respect, and the understanding that every action carries a consequence.

By the time I graduated from the alternative learning space, my reading and math skills were at college level, and I was automatically placed in college-bound classes at Walton High School as a freshman. I had learned to value knowledge, diligence, and the power of learning, seeing early that education was both a shield and a sword in the Bronx.

These early school years were more than academics — they were a laboratory for social intelligence. I learned to navigate peer groups, assert boundaries, and identify mentors. Every challenge, mistake, and success added layers to my understanding of the world. By blending lessons from the classroom with observations from the streets, I was already developing the skills, insight, and foresight that would later define my life.

Chapter 2, Part 2 — Peer Interactions & Social Lessons

From a young age, I realized that people were naturally drawn to me, whether for friendship, guidance, or influence. Even at five or six years old, I had a unique ability to connect with others — adults and children alike. My mother would often warn me before we left the house: "Remember, you have to be careful with the friends you make. Not everyone has your best interests at heart." I listened, but even then, I was already forming networks, building relationships, and learning the delicate balance of trust, loyalty, and influence.

I was probably the only five-year-old who had adult friends I could converse with for hours, play cards with, and learn from. These early interactions taught me more than school ever could. I learned how to read people, how to gauge intentions, and how to navigate social hierarchies. These skills became a cornerstone of my survival — both in the streets and in life.

Friendships were not just about play or fun; they were lessons in loyalty and accountability. I saw how some kids broke trust, how others held their word, and how a single act could elevate or ruin a reputation. This understanding guided me in choosing allies and mentors carefully, knowing that a reliable companion could make the difference between success and failure, safety and danger.

School trips, playground disputes, and casual interactions all became teaching moments. I learned early that observation and reflection were as critical as participation. Watching others make mistakes, succeed, or face consequences allowed me to internalize lessons without paying the full price myself. I began to understand the unspoken rules that governed social interactions, community respect, and influence — lessons I would carry throughout my life.

Even mundane experiences, like going for haircuts or running errands, were opportunities to observe social behavior and understand how trust, respect, and communication shaped relationships. My ability to connect, listen, and learn from these small moments built a foundation for leadership, problem-solving, and empathy.

By the time I was in middle school, these early peer interactions had taught me that influence, guidance, and loyalty were interdependent. You could lead, but only if you understood the people around you. You could trust, but only if you discerned intentions clearly. And you could survive — even thrive — only if you mastered both observation and action.

These lessons weren't abstract theories; they were hard-earned wisdom from living in a community where choices had immediate and real consequences. They became the blueprint for navigating adolescence, confronting street challenges, and later shaping my approach to music, entrepreneurship, and community leadership.

Chapter 2, Part 3 — Academic Growth & Alternative Learning

While my peers often struggled to see the value in school, I found learning to be both a challenge and a sanctuary. I thrived in the alternative learning space, where instruction wasn't based strictly on age but on ability. Teachers like Mrs. Puckerin, Mrs. Smalls/Harris, and Mr. Julius created classrooms that felt more like workshops than schools — a place where curiosity, intelligence, and ambition could flourish.

Classes were intimate, with only a handful of students per room. Lessons were tailored to each student's pace, and discipline was rooted in care and accountability. Skipping school, fighting with classmates, or misbehaving didn't just lead to a lecture; it led to swift action. Teachers and staff — often in collaboration with parents — would ensure that the lesson was internalized. Sometimes that meant a firm hand or a tough conversation, but it always came with love and guidance. I personally experienced a few of these corrective moments, and while painful at the time, they left lasting lessons about responsibility and the consequences of choices.

Beyond the academics, this environment fostered emotional intelligence and self-discipline. Students were encouraged to explore, question, and reflect. I learned how to manage frustration, build resilience, and maintain focus under pressure. These lessons weren't just about schoolwork; they were preparing me for life, teaching me that intelligence alone wasn't enough — you needed emotional and strategic awareness to survive and thrive.

By the time I graduated from the alternative learning space, my reading and math skills were college-level, which earned me automatic placement in college-bound classes at Walton High School as a freshman. I had internalized the value of education: not just as a pathway to opportunity, but as a form of protection and empowerment. The skills I developed in these early academic settings — observation, discipline, and perseverance — became tools I would later use in the streets, music, and community leadership.

This phase of my life also revealed the importance of mentorship within structured environments. The teachers and staff were more than educators — they were guides, role models, and pillars of accountability. Their belief in my potential shaped my confidence, while their insistence on responsibility shaped my character.

Looking back, I see that the alternative learning space wasn't just a school; it was a laboratory for life, teaching lessons about adaptability, focus, collaboration, and strategy. It was where I learned that success requires a balance of knowledge, discipline, and observation — lessons that would echo throughout my adolescent and adult life.

Chapter 2, Part 4 — Peer Challenges & Social Navigation

Navigating friendships and peer groups in the Bronx was as much a lesson in survival as any classroom. From a very young age, I realized that who you surrounded yourself with could determine not only your reputation but your safety and opportunities. My mother often warned me, "Choose your friends wisely — you become like the people you spend the most time with." She was right.

Even as a five- or six-year-old, I had the rare ability to attract peers from all walks of life. Some were older, some younger, some more experienced in the streets, and some just curious about the world like me. I could spend hours talking to them, learning their routines, their habits, and their tricks for navigating the city. Unlike most kids, I wasn't scared of adults or older teens. I learned early that respect and awareness could give you access to knowledge and safety that many others lacked.

In schoolyards, streets, and playgrounds, I honed the skill of reading people. Every conversation, every gesture, and every tone carried meaning. I learned who could be trusted, who was unpredictable, and who was simply seeking an opportunity to exploit someone. These observations weren't about cynicism — they were about survival, awareness, and building networks that could help me and protect me.

Peer challenges weren't always verbal; sometimes they were physical. Fights broke out over territory, respect, or misunderstandings. But there was also a competitive camaraderie — a testing ground to sharpen instincts, resilience, and strategy. I learned when to step up, when to step back, and how to negotiate without losing respect. Some friends became lifelong allies; others were fleeting, teaching temporary lessons in trust and betrayal.

Social navigation extended beyond the street and school walls. I discovered that every interaction was an opportunity to learn or teach, to expand influence, and to create leverage for myself. Simple activities — walking to the store, attending a birthday party, or even just playing cards — became lessons in observation, negotiation, and communication. I practiced diplomacy with my peers, learned to mediate conflicts, and understood the subtle power of influence and persuasion at an early age.

Even in fun or playful moments, I was conscious of reputation and perception. I noticed that peers, teachers, and even strangers assigned value based on actions, consistency, and integrity. If someone broke their word or acted out of selfishness, word would travel fast. By observing these dynamics, I built a framework for trust and loyalty that would later shape my approach to music collaborations, community leadership, and mentorship.

The cumulative effect of these experiences was a keen sense of social intelligence, far beyond what most children develop naturally. I learned how to read situations, anticipate reactions, and protect myself emotionally and physically. The

Bronx streets were my training ground, and the lessons I learned about friendship, loyalty, and discernment became the foundation for all my later successes.

Chapter 2, Part 5 — Lessons Learned & Reflections

Looking back on my early school years and neighborhood life, I realize that every experience was a lesson — often hard, sometimes painful, but always valuable. The arrests, the run-ins with authority, the conflicts with peers, and the triumphs in classrooms and on the streets weren't isolated events; they were all part of a larger education in resilience, responsibility, and strategy.

One of the biggest lessons I learned was accountability. Actions had consequences, whether immediate or delayed. When the police came to arrest me in fourth grade, or when disputes erupted over territory or respect, I understood that my choices directly influenced outcomes for myself and for others around me. It wasn't enough to react impulsively; I had to think, calculate, and anticipate the consequences of my actions.

Another lesson was the value of observation. Watching how older kids interacted, how teachers disciplined, and how neighbors responded to incidents gave me an informal education in human behavior. I learned to read expressions, tone, and body language. I saw how respect was earned, how fear could be manipulated, and how loyalty could be cultivated or broken. These lessons weren't taught in school, but they were more impactful than anything I learned from textbooks.

I also discovered the importance of adaptability. Life on the block and in school didn't follow a script. Situations changed rapidly — friends switched sides, new rules emerged in the neighborhood, and authority figures acted unpredictably. I learned to adapt quickly, to adjust strategies, and to stay focused on my goals even when circumstances were chaotic or unfair.

Equally critical was the lesson of empathy and influence. I realized that leadership wasn't about physical strength or intimidation alone. It was about understanding others, anticipating their needs and motivations, and helping guide them toward better outcomes. Whether mediating disputes among peers or mentoring younger kids on the block, I learned that influence was a tool far more powerful than brute force.

Perhaps the most enduring lesson from this time was the value of preparation and planning for the future. While other kids focused solely on the moment, I was already thinking about how experiences today would shape tomorrow. How could I use knowledge gained from missteps to avoid larger pitfalls later? How could I transform small victories into larger opportunities? This mindset became the foundation for everything I did in later life — from navigating the music industry to building my nonprofit and mentoring youth.

Reflecting on these experiences, I understand now that these early years were the crucible in which my character was forged. The streets, the schools, the peer dynamics — they were all shaping me into someone who could not only survive adversity but thrive in it. Every challenge taught resilience, every success instilled confidence, and every mistake provided a roadmap for future decisions.

Chapter 2 wasn't just about surviving childhood in the Bronx; it was about learning how to live with intention, strategy, and integrity, laying the groundwork for everything that came after. These lessons became my compass, guiding me through the complexities of adolescence, young adulthood, and ultimately, my career, my family life, and my work in the community.

Chapter 3, Part 1 — Emotional Loss & Early Trauma

The first time I truly felt the weight of loss was when my mother passed away. For years afterward, I carried a grief so heavy it felt like a physical burden. I didn't seek death by suicide, but I often found myself walking paths of extreme risk, testing boundaries, and putting myself in dangerous situations as if I were daring fate. I remember days when I was caught in two or three shootouts — separate conflicts, different people, different motives — yet they all had one shared goal: to end me.

People around me called me reckless, fearless, a "one-man gang," or even crazy. But none of them saw the emotional storm inside me. Every fight, every confrontation, every night spent wandering the streets was my way of coping with a heart shattered by loss and a mind consumed by grief. On the outside, I projected confidence, skill, and control. On the inside, I was navigating a storm that few could understand.

This period taught me resilience in its rawest form. Survival was no longer optional; it was the only path forward. I learned to calculate risk, observe human behavior, and trust only those who had proven themselves through action. The streets became a school where the lessons were cruel but necessary.

At the same time, I internalized the immense value of a person's word. I saw that honesty and trust could create opportunities even in the most chaotic circumstances. Someone keeping their word could get more credit, respect, and trust than someone with money in hand. Conversely, betrayal could be deadly. I watched lives unravel and reputations destroyed because someone broke their word. I understood that in life, the integrity of your word could mean the difference between freedom and a casket.

Even in the darkest moments, I began to notice small threads of guidance and protection from people who cared, quietly influencing my choices without preaching. These individuals showed me that even in chaos, loyalty and guidance can exist, and sometimes, that guidance saves a life more effectively than any rule, lecture, or punishment.

Chapter 3, Part 2 — Losing My Father & Lessons from Grief

When I was incarcerated in 1992, the world delivered a blow I wasn't prepared for — my father passed away. The pain was immediate and deep, cutting to the core of my being. He wasn't just a parent; he was the man who gave me life, who had quietly shaped my understanding of strength, loyalty, and responsibility. Yet, I wasn't there for him in his final moments.

I had spoken to him often on the phone, but I longed to be physically present. I wanted to see his face, to feel his hand, to share those final breaths. Instead, I was confined to a cell, helpless and powerless. It was a crushing lesson in the reality that time doesn't wait for anyone, a lesson in loss that no conversation or phone call could remedy.

Escorted by a correctional officer to his funeral, I realized the depth of my own responsibility for my life. I had put myself in a position where I could not be there for the man who had always been there for me. That experience ignited a determination that would guide every decision I made afterward: I would never again allow my choices to rob me of precious moments with those I loved.

The grief taught me another vital lesson: life is fragile, and opportunities are fleeting. I had to move through the world with intentionality, to cherish every moment with family and friends, and to create a life that honored the sacrifices of those who came before me. The streets, the incarceration, and the chaos of my early life had given me resilience, but this loss added a layer of profound emotional clarity — a recognition that some lessons could only come through pain, and some wisdom only through grief.

In those moments, I began to see patterns I had ignored before. I understood that life wasn't just about survival in the streets or excelling academically; it was about leaving a legacy, honoring those who built you, and preparing yourself for the future. The experiences of loss taught me empathy, patience, and the responsibility that comes with leadership — lessons that would carry through my music, my family life, and eventually, my work in the community.

This chapter of my life wasn't just about sorrow; it was about reflection, growth, and the internalization of lessons that would shape my choices for decades. Losing my father while I was behind bars crystallized the importance of presence, the urgency of love, and the unspoken promise I made to myself: to live a life worthy of the sacrifices, guidance, and example he had given me.

Chapter 3, Part 3 — Survival, Street Lessons & Early Incarceration

After losing both of my parents, the streets became my sanctuary and my battlefield. Life had already taught me the art of survival, but this chapter of my youth tested every lesson I had ever learned. Every day, I walked a line between resilience and recklessness, between risk and instinct, and I remember standing alone on the block, hearing the shots, feeling the emptiness. Why her? Why now? I asked myself. But I also knew I couldn't fall apart — I had to keep moving. Each step, each decision, was a chance to honor her memory. I whispered under my breath, "I'll make this work. I'll survive. I'll turn this pain into something bigger than me." between loyalty and self-preservation.

I remember vividly the sense of invincibility mixed with despair. Shootouts, fights, and confrontations were no longer sporadic; they became the rhythm of daily existence. Yet, beneath the chaos, I was learning the true meaning of consequences. Every action could result in freedom or a casket, every choice could build opportunity or destruction.

Despite the constant danger, I sought structure in the madness. My father's absence was a void that I attempted to fill with discipline — a relentless self-imposed accountability. I realized that trust and loyalty were the most valuable currency on these streets. One mistake, one broken promise, and everything could crumble. I learned early that a man's word wasn't just reputation — it was survival.

Being incarcerated taught me lessons I would carry for life. In 1992, during one of my first serious incarcerations, I witnessed firsthand how the system could strip a man of freedom, dignity, and connection. Rikers Island wasn't just a place of confinement; it was a crucible for reflection. I watched how men reacted to injustice, how some hardened themselves into bitterness while others found clarity in restraint.

I also discovered that leadership isn't assigned — it's proven. Even in the chaos of prison life, respect had to be earned through consistent action, integrity, and the courage to stand for what was right. I observed mentors, peers, and even adversaries, learning to navigate power structures with strategy rather than aggression alone.

Music and creativity became my lifeline. I poured my experiences into lyrics, crafting narratives that reflected the struggle, resilience, and aspirations of a young man growing up in the Bronx. Songs weren't just entertainment; they were declarations of survival, statements of identity, and vessels for emotion I couldn't otherwise express.

Ultimately, this period of my life cemented a philosophy that would guide me for decades: life is defined not by the challenges you face, but by how you respond to them. Street lessons, personal losses, and early encounters with the justice system taught me that survival requires vision, strategy, loyalty, and self-respect — and that those who endure with integrity leave behind a legacy far greater than any material gain.

Chapter 3, Part 4 — Reflections & Lessons Learned

Looking back on those turbulent years, I see that the streets, the early incarcerations, and the constant threats weren't just random trials — they were lessons in resilience, strategy, and morality. Each encounter taught me to read people, assess risk, and navigate situations with clarity. Every close call underscored the importance of foresight, patience, and the ability to stay calm under pressure.

I also learned that survival requires more than physical skill. Mental acuity, emotional intelligence, and strategic thinking were just as important as knowing how to defend oneself or maneuver through a fight. I realized that observing patterns, understanding motivations, and predicting outcomes could prevent harm far more effectively than brute force alone.

Perhaps the most critical lesson was about loyalty and trust. Street life might glorify independence and rebellion, but I discovered that success and safety were built on the foundation of dependable allies. A single trustworthy companion could be the difference between life and death, between success and ruin. That bond had to be nurtured with consistency, respect, and honesty — values that would later influence how I built relationships in music, business, and community work.

During this period, I also reflected on the power of words and promises. I witnessed how quickly reputations could be shattered, how betrayal could escalate violence, and how a broken promise could destroy more than just trust — it could destroy lives. Conversely, keeping one's word became a sacred form of currency, opening doors and creating opportunities where money alone could not.

These reflections shaped my approach to life in every domain: family, friendships, music, and eventually my nonprofit work. I learned that adversity could refine character, that trauma could teach empathy, and that mistakes, if analyzed and internalized, could become guiding principles.

Chapter 3, Part 5 — Transition into Young Adulthood & Turning Points

As I moved into my late teens and early twenties, the lessons of childhood and adolescence collided with the realities of adulthood. The streets, once a training ground, became a proving ground, and the choices I made would reverberate far beyond my immediate world. The losses I had endured, the arrests I had faced, and the close calls I had survived all converged into a single, undeniable truth: life demanded responsibility, foresight, and resilience.

The death of my father and the absence of my mother left a void that no adult supervision could fill. I had to learn quickly how to navigate complex social dynamics, manage risk, and assume a level of accountability far beyond my years. Every encounter on the streets, every altercation, and every strategic decision shaped me. I understood that survival required both instinct and intellect, and that those who failed to recognize the balance often fell victim to chaos.

During this time, music became more than an outlet — it became a lifeline. My partner Labru and I honed our skills daily, competing and collaborating in ways that sharpened both creativity and discipline. We battled at talent shows, wrote and rewrote lyrics until every line resonated, and learned to translate our life experiences into art. These moments weren't just performances; they were lessons in focus, resilience, and the power of storytelling. Every verse, every rhyme, was a reflection of our struggles, our triumphs, and the streets that had shaped us.

The streets themselves continued to teach — lessons in loyalty, trust, and consequence. I learned to identify true allies from opportunists, to anticipate danger before it arrived, and to act with clarity under pressure. Even the smallest interactions — sharing a meal, negotiating a deal, or mediating a dispute — became microcosms of life lessons in strategy, leadership, and human behavior.

Equally important were the internal transformations. I began to develop foresight, purpose, and vision, understanding that the choices I made today would define the man I became tomorrow. I learned that strength was not only measured by physical prowess or fearlessness, but by the capacity to endure hardship with integrity, to act with intention, and to protect those who relied on you.

Looking back, these turning points laid the foundation for everything that followed: my music career, my entrepreneurial ventures, my advocacy work, and ultimately the creation of my nonprofit, I Am My Community Inc. Each challenge, each victory, each heartbreak, was part of a larger narrative about growth, resilience, and the pursuit of purpose.

Chapter 3 closes with the understanding that young adulthood is not merely a stage of age, but a test of character. The streets, the losses, the early brushes with the justice system, and the triumphs in music all converged to forge a young man who would not only survive but begin to thrive — prepared to step into leadership, community service, and the long arc of life that awaited them.

Chapter 4, Part 1 — Street Encounters & Early Survival

As I stepped further into young adulthood, the streets became more than a backdrop — they were the stage where I learned the laws of loyalty, respect, and survival. Every corner, every block, every encounter carried lessons that no classroom could teach. From a young age, I had understood that having a trusted sidekick was essential. Someone who could move with you, cover your back, and share the burden of risk. Labru was that person for me. We were inseparable, bonded by trust, shared experience, and a mutual understanding that loyalty was non-negotiable.

Every day with Labru was a lesson in discipline and competitive excellence. We battled each other in rap contests not just for money, but to sharpen our craft. Music became our arena for testing skills, creativity, and resilience. One evening at the world-famous Disco Fever in the Bronx, I won first place while Labru came in second. That night, as we split the prize money, we were observed by DJ Starchild, who would later introduce us to a network that connected us to Teddy Riley and Gusto Wells — a pivotal moment that transformed our music trajectory.

But survival wasn't only about music. It was about understanding the unspoken rules of the streets. I learned that being a hustler meant more than selling product; it meant honoring your word, planning ahead, and building strategies for both immediate gain and long-term stability. Many so-called hustlers around me ended up broke, not because of lack of skill, but because they failed to plan, failed to honor commitments, and failed to think beyond the moment. Real hustling required vision.

I also learned early that danger could come from any direction. Conflicts arose unexpectedly, alliances shifted, and authority figures were often unpredictable. These experiences demanded not only physical skill but mental acuity and strategic thinking. I observed, calculated, and adapted constantly. Every interaction — whether a dispute over respect, a negotiation for resources, or a clash of rival groups — was a test of judgment and foresight.

The streets also reinforced the value of mentorship and guidance. Older figures, experienced in both the harsh realities of urban life and the complexities of human behavior, served as informal teachers. They offered insights, cautionary tales, and wisdom that, while hard-earned, became invaluable tools for navigating both music and life. I realized that knowledge and experience could be leveraged as a weapon and a shield — sometimes even more powerful than physical force.

Ultimately, these street encounters were more than just survival exercises; they were training in leadership, resilience, and strategic thinking. They prepared me for the responsibilities I would later take on in music, in community work, and in my personal life. Each challenge faced and each obstacle overcome was a lesson in self-reliance, the importance of relationships, and the value of integrity in a world where trust was scarce.

Chapter 4, Part 2 — Music, Mentorship & Rising Opportunities

While the streets taught lessons in survival and strategy, music became my compass, guiding me through chaos toward something purposeful. Labru and I spent countless hours writing, rehearsing, and battling — not just for victory in the moment, but to sharpen our skills for the opportunities that awaited. Each rhyme, each verse, and each freestyle was a test of creativity, discipline, and focus.

Our first major breakthrough came at Disco Fever, a legendary Bronx venue where talent was showcased and reputations were forged. Winning first place in a talent contest, with Labru following closely behind, was more than just a prize — it was validation. DJ Starchild noticed our potential and connected us to the larger network of artists and producers, ultimately introducing us to D.J. Brucie B, Teddy Riley, and Gusto Wells. These connections marked a pivotal turning point, bridging street credibility with professional opportunity.

Mentorship played an essential role in our journey. Teddy Riley, already pioneering the New Jack Swing movement, didn't just provide production expertise — he became a teacher, showing us how to structure songs, arrange harmonies, and convey stories through music. With each session in the studio, I internalized not just technical skills, but lessons in professionalism, collaboration, and creative integrity.

Beyond music, mentorship included lessons in business and strategy. Labru and I were shown the importance of branding, presentation, and networking. The streets had taught us loyalty and trust, but the music industry required negotiation, foresight, and long-term planning. These lessons would become invaluable as we navigated record deals, endorsements, and promotional opportunities.

During this period, I also began to understand the importance of balancing ambition with responsibility. Music offered the promise of fame and financial reward, but it also demanded time, focus, and dedication. Each decision — which gigs to take, which collaborators to trust, and how to present ourselves — carried consequences that could either propel us forward or hinder our progress. The discipline we learned in school and on the streets became critical to making smart, sustainable choices.

The Recording Studio Moment

The smell of fresh vinyl, the hum of the mixing board — I could feel the pulse of every beat. Labru and I locked eyes, silently daring each other to bring our best. This wasn't just about winning a talent show anymore; it was about staking our claim, making a mark, leaving a legacy. Every note, every lyric, carried the weight of my upbringing, my struggles, and my dreams.

Finally, the opportunities we seized were amplified by the systems and structures we built. We documented lyrics, rehearsed regularly, and maintained a schedule that mirrored professional expectations. This approach allowed us to scale our impact, prepare for performances, and consistently deliver quality work. It taught me that success is rarely accidental — it is constructed through careful planning, mentorship, and deliberate action.

Music became more than a career pathway — it became a framework for growth, mentorship, and leadership. It was proof that lessons from the streets, family, and peers could converge to create a life with purpose, direction, and opportunity. Chapter 4 was not just about surviving young adulthood; it was about leveraging talent, relationships, and discipline to carve out a path for the future.

Chapter 4, Part 3 — Hustling, Risk, and Strategic Thinking

Life on the streets was never simple. Every day brought opportunities, challenges, and decisions that could define your path — sometimes for years to come. I quickly realized that hustling was more than moving product or making money; it was an exercise in strategy, trust, and long-term planning.

From my earliest experiences, I understood that success required discipline and foresight. The streets rewarded those who honored commitments, anticipated challenges, and built relationships wisely. A man's word was currency — more valuable than cash in the pocket — because reputation and trust determined whether you survived and thrived.

I also discovered that hustling was a game of scaling opportunities while minimizing risk. Observing peers and rivals, I learned that many who called themselves "hustlers" were actually short-term operators — individuals who worked without a plan, consumed gains recklessly, and ultimately failed. A real hustler measured the long-term impact of each move, built networks carefully, and invested in skills, relationships, and opportunities that could compound over time.

Labru and I applied these lessons not just to street business but also to music. Every performance, every battle, every recording session was a negotiation in strategy. We learned to maximize opportunities, divide resources effectively, and capitalize on timing. The discipline and intelligence required to navigate the streets translated directly into how we approached music, business, and life.

Risk management became a core part of my identity. Whether handling conflict on a corner or negotiating a deal in the studio, I learned to assess every situation for threats, advantages, and potential outcomes. Survival wasn't about avoiding risk entirely — it was about controlling risk, making calculated moves, and knowing when to act or wait.

Beyond strategy and money, I absorbed the importance of mentorship and example. Younger kids on the block watched how Labru and I conducted ourselves, learning about integrity, decision-making, and the consequences of actions. Hustling, for me, was about more than profit; it was teaching leadership, responsibility, and foresight by example.

These lessons shaped the foundation for later stages of my life: the music industry, entrepreneurial ventures, and eventually, my work with I Am My Community Inc. Chapter 4, Part 3 reminds me that every decision carries weight, and the principles learned during these formative years — strategy, trust, risk assessment, and mentorship — would guide me through adulthood and help me build lasting impact.

Chapter 4, Part 4 — Music, Legacy, and Community Lessons

By the time we were recording New Generation with Teddy Riley and Gusto Wells, I began to understand that music was far more than entertainment — it was a tool to express, influence, and uplift. The streets had taught me survival, strategy, and loyalty, but music taught me voice, vision, and the power of storytelling. Every lyric we wrote reflected experiences that were raw, real, and rooted in the realities of Bronx life: the struggles, the triumphs, the heartbreak, and the hope.

The process of creating music was itself an education in discipline, patience, and collaboration. We spent hours in the studio, perfecting verses, harmonies, and flows. Each session required focus, creativity, and a willingness to be challenged. Teddy Riley, a master of the New Jack Swing sound, demanded precision but also encouraged experimentation. He taught me that innovation requires both skill and fearless authenticity.

Beyond technical mastery, music offered lessons in legacy and influence. I realized that what we created could inspire, provoke thought, and even guide others. Songs weren't just personal victories; they were tools for shaping community perception and identity. This understanding sparked a larger awareness: every action, every decision, every word carries weight — whether on the streets, in the studio, or in the community.

I also began to see the role of mentorship and giving back. As we gained recognition, younger artists looked to us as examples. Labru and I made it a priority to support aspiring musicians, guide peers, and share knowledge that could help them navigate both the industry and life. It wasn't about fame or money; it was about responsibility, influence, and building a foundation for others to thrive.

The experience of music taught me about legacy beyond personal achievement. Success isn't measured solely by accolades or wealth, but by the impact one leaves on people, culture, and community. This perspective would later inform how I structured my nonprofit, I Am My Community Inc, ensuring that programs for youth were rooted in lessons of integrity, opportunity, and empowerment.

Finally, this period reinforced a truth I had learned early on the streets: structure and systems amplify impact. Whether in music, business, or community service, creating frameworks that endure beyond individual effort is key. Every mentorship program, every workshop, and every initiative we built became a blueprint for sustained positive influence — a lesson that would carry me into the next chapters of life, where advocacy and service became central to my purpose.

Chapter 4, Part 5 — Reflections & Foreshadowing: Laying the Groundwork for Service & Advocacy

Looking back on this period, I can see how the lessons of streets, survival, and music converged to prepare me for a larger purpose. It wasn't enough to survive or even to thrive personally — I realized that true impact required giving back, building structures, and leading with intention. Every challenge, every close call, and every milestone in music contributed to a blueprint for service that would guide my later work with youth and my community.

The streets had taught me the hard truths of loyalty, trust, and consequence. Music had taught me the power of voice, discipline, and vision. Together, these experiences instilled an understanding that real leadership is not self-serving — it is about creating opportunities for others to rise. I began to think not just about my path, but about how I could influence the next generation, how I could turn experiences of hardship into tools for empowerment.

Reflections during this period also emphasized the importance of systems and consistency. I understood that individual actions, while meaningful, were limited in scope. Lasting change required structures — programs that could operate independently, mentorship systems that could reach beyond my immediate presence, and processes that could scale without losing integrity. This foresight would become essential when establishing I Am My Community Inc, ensuring that youth could benefit from consistent guidance, resources, and support regardless of my direct involvement.

Foreshadowing the next chapter, these lessons formed the foundation for service, advocacy, and leadership. The streets, music, and survival strategies had all been practice for something bigger: designing a life that could transform communities, empower youth, and provide alternatives to cycles of violence and neglect. Every decision in this period — from how I built my network in music to how I mentored peers — was laying groundwork for the chapters ahead, where advocacy would become as central to my identity as survival had been.

Ultimately, Chapter 4 closes with the understanding that preparation meets opportunity. The lessons learned — loyalty, strategy, mentorship, and systems thinking — were all precursors to a life dedicated not just to personal achievement, but to lifting others and building sustainable impact. The streets, the studios, and the challenges had equipped me to step confidently into a role as a guide, a mentor, and a leader for the generations that would follow.

A Note for the Next Generation

Dear Ones,

Life will try to knock you down before you even know how to walk. But remember: every setback is a lesson. Loyalty, respect, and accountability are your foundation. If you ever lose your way, look back at the people who have guided you and the lessons they've taught. And know that your actions — small or large — ripple far beyond what you see

Chapter 5, Part 1 — Daily Routines, Discipline, and Values

Once I became a father, my daily life shifted into a rhythm of responsibility that far surpassed anything I had known on the streets or in the studio. Each morning began with getting my children ready for school, ensuring they were nourished, prepared, and mentally ready for the day ahead. This routine was not just a duty — it was a lesson in consistency, accountability, and intentionality. My actions were not for me alone; they modeled behavior, instilled values, and created a standard that my children could emulate.

I taught them early that association shapes identity. Hanging out with peers who lacked ambition or integrity would naturally pull them into similar patterns. Conversely, surrounding oneself with disciplined, motivated, and trustworthy people opened doors, fostered growth, and instilled confidence. From a young age, my children understood that success required both effort and selective association — lessons I had painfully learned through my own trials on the streets.

The responsibilities of fatherhood were compounded by the lessons I had learned in school, music, and survival. I stressed education as non-negotiable, emphasizing that they could leverage knowledge in ways I wished I had at their age. While I had been arrested over 77 times, I made it clear that there was no need for them to repeat my mistakes — their path could be measured, disciplined, and purposeful. I taught them to ask questions, seek knowledge, and respect their own potential, regardless of the obstacles that life might place in their way.

Rules in our home were clear and uncompromising. No drugs, no cigarettes, no tolerance for behaviors that would compromise integrity or safety. These weren't just household rules; they were the foundation for a moral framework. My family and friends knew these boundaries, so there was no confusion or conflict. Boundaries like these created security, accountability, and an environment where values were taught through both example and expectation.

Beyond logistics and rules, I sought to impart the larger lessons of resilience, emotional intelligence, and foresight. Fatherhood demanded reflection, patience, and strategic thinking. I wanted my children to understand the consequences of decisions, the importance of loyalty, and the value of integrity — lessons I had internalized in music, on the streets, and during periods of hardship.

Even as a teenager myself when my first daughter was born, I embraced responsibility. Early fatherhood accelerated my growth, forcing me to balance ambition, survival, and love, and to transform life experiences into actionable wisdom. Each moment — from packing lunches to attending school events, from bedtime stories to real conversations about choices and consequences — reinforced a core principle: discipline and love are inseparable in building character and preparing for the world.

Chapter 5, Part 2 — Parenting Challenges & Street Wisdom

Parenting in the Bronx was never just about feeding, clothing, or transporting children. It was about teaching resilience in the face of systemic obstacles, instilling morality in a world that often rewarded shortcuts, and preparing young minds for the harsh realities that existed beyond the classroom and the front door. I wanted my children to navigate the streets safely, not by avoiding life, but by understanding it — by learning strategy, awareness, and integrity.

My experiences as a young man gave me perspective. I knew how the wrong environment, careless friendships, or even a single lapse in judgment could lead to disastrous outcomes. When my kids asked questions about the world, I didn't shield them from truth; I shared stories and lessons. I told them about the consequences of poor choices, about loyalty and betrayal, and about the importance of honor even when no one was watching. Every anecdote became a teaching moment, turning memories of risk, survival, and mistakes into wisdom for them.

Balancing fatherhood and community responsibility meant sacrifices and calculations. Every time I took a child to a school event or a community program, I weighed the benefits of exposure, mentorship, and guidance against the unpredictable dangers of the streets. But I refused to let fear dictate our experiences. I believed that courage guided by knowledge created stronger children, capable of making their own informed decisions while retaining respect for rules, safety, and community.

Incorporating street wisdom into parenting meant I was honest about danger. I explained how alliances worked, why trust is precious, and why a person's word is more valuable than gold or cash. I taught them that the streets could be navigated safely if one observed patterns, respected rules, and aligned with trustworthy allies. These were not lessons to instill fear but to empower them with clarity and foresight.

Discipline in our household extended beyond rules. It was about accountability, reflection, and planning. When a child made a mistake, I didn't simply punish; I guided them to understand the implications, correct behavior, and make better decisions next time. Each lesson reinforced the principle that responsibility is not just a duty but a practice of character, and that every choice carries weight in shaping life's trajectory.

Parenting was also about modeling resilience. I demonstrated how to rise after failure, take ownership of mistakes, and remain focused under pressure. From managing daily routines to handling conflicts with patience and strategy, my children observed actions paired with principles — lessons I hoped would stick long after childhood.

Chapter 5, Part 3 — Teaching Values Through Daily Actions

Parenting is not a set of abstract lessons; it is lived experience, repeated day after day, in every small choice, gesture, and moment of presence. I wanted my children to understand values through observation and repetition, not just through words. Every morning when I helped them get ready for school, every homework session, every conversation on the way to appointments became an opportunity to embed principles of responsibility, respect, and accountability.

I stressed the importance of self-discipline early on. Whether it was managing time, saving money, or completing tasks without being reminded, these were small habits that compounded into life-long skills. I taught them to understand cause and effect: if they skipped a responsibility, there would be consequences; if they honored commitments, they would earn trust and opportunities. Lessons were consistent and tangible, grounded in the realities of life I had lived.

But discipline alone wasn't enough. I wanted my children to internalize respect and empathy. Respect for elders, peers, and even those they might disagree with. Empathy for those struggling or in need. I encouraged them to observe not only their own actions but the effect those actions had on others, and to recognize that true strength came not from dominance or intimidation, but from compassion, fairness, and integrity.

Street lessons also shaped how I approached these teachings. I shared stories of loyalty, betrayal, and survival, not to glorify danger but to illustrate the real consequences of choices. I explained how a single misstep, a broken promise, or an unwise association could escalate quickly, sometimes with lifelong consequences. Conversely, I showed how a commitment to honesty, fairness, and follow-through could open doors that money alone could not.

Music and creative expression became tools for teaching as well. I encouraged my children to write, rap, or tell stories about their experiences and observations. Through these outlets, they practiced self-reflection, communication, and problem-solving, turning daily experiences into lessons in personal development. I emphasized that every story, every verse, and every word had power — and that they could choose to use that power to inspire, educate, or uplift others, just as I had learned to do in my own youth.

I also taught financial literacy and planning. From splitting allowances to understanding how to save for future goals, I wanted my children to recognize that money, while necessary, is a tool — not an end. The principles of budgeting, investing in education, and preparing for opportunities were habits designed to give them independence and stability, lessons I had learned painfully in my own life.

Ultimately, Chapter 5, Part 3 is about modeling values consistently, with presence, patience, and intentionality. It is about showing through action that integrity, discipline, empathy, and foresight are not abstract ideas, but practices woven into daily life. By embedding these lessons in routine, observation, and example, I ensured that my children could navigate the world with confidence, wisdom, and resilience, carrying forward principles that I had lived, learned, and refined through years of experience.

Chapter 5, Part 4 — Reflection & Foreshadowing for Service & Advocacy

Parenting is more than teaching children to read, write, or behave. It is about instilling values that endure beyond the immediate moment, lessons that can shape a life, a community, and ultimately, a legacy. As I reflect on the years raising my children, guiding them through school, extracurricular activities, and the daily challenges of growing up in the Bronx, I realize that every lesson, every conversation, and every consistent action was preparing me for the work I would do beyond my family — for the community I would come to serve.

The routines, the boundaries, the insistence on accountability — these were not just rules; they were training in leadership, responsibility, and long-term thinking. Every morning that I woke my kids, ensured they were fed, prepared for school, and mentally ready for the day, I was practicing skills I would later use to organize community programs, mentor youth, and build a nonprofit. Teaching them about loyalty, honesty, and resilience mirrored the larger lessons needed for any community to thrive.

Raising children in a complex environment taught me that structure is everything. Without routines, guidance, and consistent expectations, even the most capable young people can falter. It became clear to me that community work operates on the same principle: programs must be intentional, repeatable, and sustainable. Mentorship initiatives, youth workshops, and after-school programs are most effective when they have clear rules, trained facilitators, and measurable outcomes — just like parenting requires planning, patience, and follow-through.

Parenting also reinforced the idea of extended family and community as safety nets. I saw the ways that children could flourish when adults around them provided guidance, resources, and support. This lesson shaped my vision for I Am My Community Inc, where the goal was not merely to intervene in crises but to create systems that empower youth, teach accountability, and foster a sense of belonging. Each child's success, each life positively influenced, became a testament to the power of structure, mentorship, and intentional guidance.

Foreshadowing the next chapter, it becomes evident that the skills and principles honed in the home — patience, observation, discipline, and consistent teaching — naturally transitioned into community leadership. The experiences of guiding children, setting boundaries, and nurturing growth became the blueprint for building programs that could operate at scale, impact generations, and create sustainable change. It was no longer enough to survive or even to thrive personally; I understood that my influence could extend far beyond my immediate family, shaping neighborhoods, opportunities, and futures for those who had no one else to guide them.

This chapter closes with the understanding that parenting and community service are inseparable in purpose. Every small act of guidance at home mirrors the work of advocacy in the community. Every lesson imparted to a child — about responsibility, resilience, or loyalty — reflects the principles needed to uplift and strengthen the broader society. The reflections here set the stage for Chapter 6, where service and advocacy become central, transforming lived experience into structured programs, mentorship, and meaningful impact across the Bronx and beyond.

Chapter 6, Part 1 — Launching I Am My Community Inc

The decision to start I Am My Community Inc did not come overnight. It was the culmination of decades of experience — the streets, the classrooms, the studios, the challenges, and the triumphs — all converging into a single purpose: to give back, to guide, and to create opportunities where none existed. I had seen what happened when youth went without guidance: potential squandered, lives cut short, dreams deferred. I knew that a single conversation, a single intervention, could redirect a trajectory that otherwise might have ended in tragedy.

Starting the nonprofit required a combination of vision, planning, and relentless action. I wanted more than an organization that merely existed; I wanted one that worked, adapted, and empowered. The first step was understanding the community's needs. I walked the streets, visited local schools, and spoke with parents, teachers, and youth leaders. Every conversation confirmed what I already knew in my heart: young people needed mentorship, structure, and exposure to positive role models and resources.

The first programs were simple but intentional. We held weekly mentorship circles, giving youth a safe space to talk about challenges, aspirations, and fears. I invited artists, entrepreneurs, and community leaders to share their experiences, demonstrating that success and integrity were achievable. Sports leagues became a platform for teamwork, discipline, and leadership, while food pantries ensured that children had their most basic needs met. Every initiative reinforced a principle I had learned early: opportunity is only as powerful as the structure that supports it.

Building the organization also required understanding the mechanics of sustainability. Volunteers had to be trained, protocols had to be established, and outcomes had to be measurable. I implemented systems for tracking participation, engagement, and progress, ensuring that every program could operate independently yet remain effective. I wanted I Am My Community Inc to endure — to thrive long after my immediate presence, and to touch generations of youth who might never meet me in person.

The work also brought lessons in humility and collaboration. I quickly learned that change does not happen in isolation. Partnerships with schools, local businesses, city agencies, and other nonprofits were essential. Each relationship required negotiation, patience, and trust. I realized that being a leader meant aligning resources, people, and vision — ensuring that everyone involved shared a commitment to integrity, accountability, and empowerment.

Launching I Am My Community Inc was not without challenges. Funding was scarce, skepticism was high, and bureaucratic obstacles were constant. Yet, the energy of the youth, the gratitude of parents, and the small wins in the community reinforced the mission. I understood that impact is cumulative, and that even the smallest intervention — a conversation, a workshop, a mentorship moment — could ripple outward to create profound change.

This part of the story closes with the awareness that service is both a responsibility and a privilege. I Am My Community Inc became the physical manifestation of everything I had learned: the importance of structure, mentorship, loyalty, resilience, and strategic thinking. It was the culmination of street wisdom, life experience, and the desire to ensure that the next generation would have opportunities I wished I had at their age.

Chapter 6, Part 2 — Expanding Programs and Community Impact

Once I Am My Community Inc was established, the next step was to scale its reach while maintaining quality and intention. Starting with a handful of programs and a few committed volunteers, I realized quickly that the youth, families, and neighborhoods needed more than temporary interventions — they needed continuity, structure, and access to resources that could change the trajectory of their lives.

The first expansion involved after-school programs. These were designed to give children and teens a safe space to study, explore creative outlets, and build skills beyond the classroom. I brought in mentors from music, art, sports, and entrepreneurship, each trained to not only teach but also model integrity, discipline, and resilience. Every session reinforced principles I had learned firsthand: teamwork, respect, and the consequences of choices.

Sports programs became a cornerstone of community engagement. Beyond the obvious health and fitness benefits, leagues and tournaments were microcosms of life lessons. Players learned strategy, accountability, and how to navigate competition while respecting rules and authority. Wins and losses became teaching moments; discipline on the field translated into self-discipline off the field.

Food security programs followed, addressing a fundamental barrier to success: hunger. I implemented weekly food pantries and meal distributions that served hundreds of families. Each event reinforced community bonds and highlighted the importance of giving and receiving help with

dignity. The youth learned that support is a two-way street —
that helping others is as important as being helped.

I also developed mentorship pipelines to ensure long-term
impact. Older youth who had benefited from the programs
were invited to mentor younger participants, creating a culture
of peer leadership and responsibility. This structure allowed
lessons to be reinforced and scaled, building a network of
leaders within the community who understood firsthand the
challenges and opportunities their peers faced.

Partnerships with schools, local businesses, and city
agencies were crucial. These collaborations provided
resources, venues, and visibility, while also teaching the
youth about professionalism, networking, and accountability.
By connecting the programs to the broader infrastructure of
the city, I ensured that impact could be measurable,
sustainable, and replicable.

Throughout this expansion, one principle remained at the
center: all programming must empower youth to see
themselves as capable, resilient, and worthy of opportunity.
Every workshop, every mentorship session, and every event
was designed with this goal in mind. The focus was never on
temporary entertainment or quick fixes — it was about
building character, confidence, and competence.

Chapter 6, Part 2 ends with the understanding that service and advocacy are ongoing processes, requiring adaptation, patience, and relentless commitment. The programs were growing, the community was responding, and I was learning alongside every participant. The work was demanding, but the rewards — seeing a child succeed, witnessing a teen find their voice, knowing a family's basic needs were met — were immeasurable.

Chapter 6, Part 3 — Developing Independent Systems

I quickly realized that passion alone was not enough. Energy and good intentions could spark change, but lasting transformation required systems that could survive without me standing over every detail. I began designing every program with intention: every mentorship circle, every after-school activity, every sports league needed structure, rules, and purpose that could outlast a single person's presence.

Volunteers were trained not just to fill roles, but to understand the why behind every action. They learned to observe, guide, and correct without breaking the spirit of the youth. Each protocol, each schedule, and every procedure was built to encourage independence, responsibility, and accountability — not just for the volunteers, but for the participants themselves.

I watched as older kids who had been part of the programs for years began to step into mentorship roles. They carried the lessons forward, not because they were told to, but because they internalized the principles. A boy who had once struggled to attend class began guiding younger students on homework and etiquette. A young woman who had lacked confidence now led art workshops, encouraging her peers to express themselves. The systems allowed their growth to multiply, creating leaders who could inspire without my constant intervention.

Every activity was a carefully orchestrated lesson. Sports became more than competition; they were laboratories for discipline, teamwork, and trust. Workshops were more than instruction; they were arenas where creativity and problem-solving flourished. Even something as simple as a weekly circle of conversation was carefully planned to teach listening, expression, and empathy, with opportunities to practice negotiation, resolve conflicts, and celebrate achievements.

Building these systems was a lesson in patience. Things did not always run smoothly. Mistakes were inevitable, from volunteers forgetting steps to kids testing boundaries. But every setback was an opportunity to refine the process, to reinforce values, and to teach resilience. Slowly, the organization became a living ecosystem, one that could adapt, grow, and thrive, independent of a single person's presence.

Through it all, I learned that leadership is not about doing everything yourself. It is about creating frameworks where others can thrive, where trust and discipline are embedded in the structure, and where impact can expand far beyond a single moment or interaction. I began to see the organization not as mine alone, but as a vessel for the community — capable of empowering youth, inspiring volunteers, and changing neighborhoods.

By the end of this stage, the programs had taken on a life of their own. I could step back slightly and watch the youth succeed, the volunteers guide, and the systems hold. The streets, the mentors, and the lessons of my past had converged into something tangible, scalable, and transformative, something that promised to endure and shape lives for years to come.

Chapter 6, Part 4 — Community Leadership & Long-Term Impact

Leadership is not defined by the size of a crowd or the title on a door; it is defined by the ripples of change that spread from one act of purpose to the lives of many. As the programs of I Am My Community Inc grew, I began to see the subtle ways in which influence shaped behavior, created opportunities, and instilled confidence in those who had long been overlooked.

Walking through the streets, I could feel the impact of what we had built. Kids who once roamed corners aimlessly were now mentoring younger peers, teaching them what I had spent years teaching my own children: responsibility, respect, and foresight. The same youth who had once avoided school were now leaders in after-school workshops, guiding creative projects, and organizing sports leagues. I watched as community ownership blossomed, and for the first time, I realized that the organization was bigger than me.

With each passing year, the network of volunteers and mentors grew stronger. Adults who had once doubted the potential of our programs began to participate actively, share resources, and contribute ideas, reinforcing the principles I had built into the system. Parents expressed gratitude, neighbors began to collaborate, and schools acknowledged the value of having a consistent, structured presence for students outside of the classroom. The change was subtle, gradual, and yet undeniable — a community learning to sustain itself through trust, accountability, and shared purpose.

I also recognized the importance of celebrating achievements, no matter how small. Graduation ceremonies, award nights, and public showcases became moments to honor effort, dedication, and growth. These celebrations were more than recognition; they were evidence that the systems we built could nurture excellence, resilience, and pride. A young man who had struggled with discipline now stood in front of his peers, giving a speech about his journey and the lessons he learned from mentoring programs. A young woman who had once lacked confidence now led a workshop, her voice steady and empowered, inspiring others to follow her example.

Through this work, I began to understand that leadership is not about directing others constantly; it is about equipping people with tools, guidance, and confidence to lead themselves. The youth became teachers, the volunteers became strategists, and the community became a living, evolving ecosystem. The programs no longer required my constant presence to function because we had built a culture of responsibility, initiative, and collaboration.

By the end of this phase, I could reflect on the magnitude of what had been accomplished: a community empowered, youth inspired, and structures designed to last. I had taken lessons from my past — the streets, the mentors, the failures, and the triumphs — and turned them into a blueprint for sustainable impact. Leadership, I realized, is not measured in titles or recognition, but in the enduring strength, confidence, and vision of those you serve.

Chapter 6, Part 5 — Forward Vision & Legacy

Even as programs thrived and youth found purpose, I knew that true leadership and service were about foresight — about building for the future, not just reacting to the present. I began to think not only about the children in the room today, but about those who would walk through our doors in ten, twenty, or thirty years. The work had to be sustainable, scalable, and adaptable, capable of standing the test of time.

I focused on developing future leaders from within the community. Older youth, who had grown under our guidance, were invited to mentor and train the next generation. They were not just following instructions; they were learning to think strategically, solve problems, and inspire others. This approach created a ripple effect: those who had once needed guidance were now providing it, ensuring continuity and longevity of the mission.

Legacy meant embedding values deeply. Every decision, every program design, and every community partnership was rooted in principles that I had learned the hard way: integrity, loyalty, accountability, and foresight. I wanted every participant, volunteer, and partner to internalize these values, so that they could carry them forward into their families, workplaces, and neighborhoods. The goal was not temporary success — it was lasting transformation.

Part of building this legacy was documenting, systematizing, and sharing what worked. Training manuals, volunteer handbooks, and structured program outlines became essential. These resources allowed anyone stepping into the organization to understand, adopt, and enhance the programs without relying solely on my presence. The organization became greater than any single person, a living entity designed to empower the community for generations.

At the same time, I cultivated a vision for advocacy beyond programming. I engaged with local schools, city agencies, and other nonprofits, advocating for policies and initiatives that aligned with the lessons learned on the streets. I knew that lasting change required systemic influence, not just individual mentorship. By creating partnerships and networks, I ensured that the voices of youth and community members were heard, and that opportunities for growth were expanded far beyond our immediate reach.

Forward vision also meant looking inward, reflecting on what legacy I wanted to leave as a human being. I wanted my children and grandchildren, my community, and the youth I served to know that commitment, integrity, and love for others were the markers of a meaningful life. Every story shared, every program implemented, and every life touched became part of a continuum — a testament to what could be achieved when one chooses to serve with purpose.

As I stood at the threshold of this chapter, I understood that legacy was not a single achievement or accolade. It was the lives improved, the lessons taught, and the systems built to empower generations. It was about creating a foundation strong enough that even when I was gone, the work would continue, thriving in the hands of those inspired to carry it forward.

Chapter 7, Part 1 — The Blackout and the Streets

2004.   The city was tense. News reports warned of a blackout later that day, and I was living in the projects on 170th and Washington Avenue. My youngest daughter had just been born, and every decision I made had to account for her safety and well-being. Even small choices felt monumental.

That afternoon, my baby mother went uptown to visit a friend. She left her phone behind, and I knew I had no other way to contact her. I had to get to her before the darkness fell, before the streets became unpredictable. Walking through the block, I noticed how quiet the city felt — almost like it was holding its breath, anticipating the chaos to come. The hum of the streets, the scent of food from corner vendors, the occasional shout from a passing car — it all seemed amplified in that looming darkness.

I was only five minutes uptown when a police car pulled up behind me, sirens silent but lights flashing faintly. They approached quickly and instructed me to get in. My mind raced. Why me? Why now? I had no outstanding reason to be stopped, no immediate threat, nothing on record that should have drawn attention.

Once inside the precinct, I was processed and placed in a cell. The officers left to handle the emergency elsewhere. Minutes passed like hours. I kept my composure, but the uncertainty gnawed at me. Who knew why I was here? What charges would they claim? Then a female officer returned and, with a tremor in her voice, revealed what had me frozen in disbelief: I was being held for murder.

I remember standing there, trying to make sense of it. My mind replayed every detail: the apartment, the streets, the people I had passed. Nothing connected. No lineups, no witnesses, no court date — just a name and a charge. Fear and disbelief collided with the instinct to protect myself and my daughter. My thoughts raced: How could this happen? How could a system so massive, so seemingly meticulous, allow for this kind of error?

The first hours on Rikers Island were surreal. The weight of incarceration, even for something I did not commit, was suffocating. I observed the men around me — some hardened by years, others like me, shocked and unsure. It was a lesson in human behavior under pressure: some showed solidarity, some avoided attention, and some tested the limits of control. I learned quickly that survival required patience, observation, and restraint.

Even in the chaos, my thoughts never left my daughter. Every echo of the clanging cell doors reminded me of the fragility of life and freedom. I swore to myself that no matter what came next, I would emerge stronger, wiser, and ready to fight for justice with clarity, not anger.

The blackout loomed outside, but inside those walls, time moved differently. Minutes stretched into hours, and hours into days. Each moment was a test — a test of endurance, self-control, and mental fortitude. I realized that true strength is measured not by brute force, but by the ability to maintain integrity under impossible circumstances.

That night, the city went dark, and the streets I knew so well became a shadowed landscape of uncertainty. Yet inside me, a different kind of light burned: a determination that no matter how unjust or overwhelming the system appeared, I would navigate it, survive it, and turn the experience into lessons that could guide others.

By dawn, the first part of this chapter in my life had passed — a crucible that tested my instincts, my judgment, and my resilience. It was only the beginning of a series of events that would shape my understanding of justice, responsibility, and leadership in ways that I would carry for the rest of my life.

Chapter 7, Part 2 — The Rikers Experience

Rikers Island. Just saying the name sent chills through me, but now I was inside, and there was no escaping the reality. The gates, the razor wire, the distant shouts — everything felt designed to strip you of control, to remind you of the world you had just entered. I wasn't there for something I had done, yet the weight of the environment pressed down on me as though I had committed the gravest crimes imaginable.

The first day was an orientation in survival. Every man in the cellhouse was sizing you up, and every glance carried unspoken rules. The stories I had heard about Rikers didn't capture the rhythm of fear, vigilance, and careful observation that governed every second. You learned quickly: every word you spoke, every movement you made, could determine whether you became invisible or a target.

I observed my surroundings with acute attention. Men who appeared calm were often the most dangerous; those who shouted the loudest were often the most vulnerable. The dynamic was subtle, almost invisible to the untrained eye.

Here, the ability to read a room, gauge intent, and act deliberately wasn't optional — it was survival.

I was escorted to a cell shared with two others. Silence was the currency at first; conversation came slowly, measured, until trust began to form. Over time, I realized that the people who were able to maintain dignity under pressure were also the ones who endured, the ones who carried themselves with a quiet authority that needed no recognition. I studied them, learning not just how to survive physically, but how to navigate the psychology of confinement.

Daily routines became both a lifeline and a lesson. The monotony of meals, the regimented movements, the endless roll calls — each repetition offered a chance to observe patterns, anticipate outcomes, and exercise self-discipline. In this rigid world, I found pockets of control where I could preserve my identity, where my thoughts and intentions remained my own.

I also witnessed the consequences of choices firsthand. Some men were consumed by anger, others by despair, and some by manipulation of those around them. In every interaction, there was a lesson: loyalty, honesty, and integrity were often more valuable than brute strength. These were the same principles I had tried to instill in my community outside, now mirrored in the microcosm of incarceration.

Evenings brought reflection. The city outside was dark, disconnected from me, and I felt the fragility of freedom in ways I never had before. Yet, amid the fear and uncertainty, I discovered resilience. Every day on Rikers became a mirror: if I could maintain my composure, my principles, and my sense of purpose here, I could navigate any challenge outside those walls.

I began to write in my mind — stories, lessons, plans, visions of how to turn this ordeal into wisdom. I thought about the youth I had worked with, the future programs, the families depending on me. Every experience on Rikers became fuel, a lesson in strategy, patience, and long-term thinking.

By the end of my time in that cellhouse, I realized Rikers Island was not just a place of punishment — it was a crucible, refining the way I thought about justice, leadership, and accountability. It was shaping me not into someone hardened by fear, but into someone capable of transforming experience into guidance, and pain into purpose.

Chapter 7, Part 3 — The Grand Jury and Legal Challenges

After my time on Rikers Island, I was brought before the grand jury. Walking into that courtroom, I felt the weight of every accusation, every assumption, and every expectation bearing down on me. It wasn't just about the law — it was about how the system viewed someone like me: a young Black man from the Bronx, familiar with the streets, and now caught in a machinery that seemed indifferent to truth.

The grand jury process was unlike anything I had ever experienced. Questions were asked that assumed guilt rather than explored fact. I answered honestly, and repeatedly, clarifying that I had never been in a lineup, never participated in any prior investigation, and never had a chance to defend myself in the ways others could take for granted. Every answer was met with skepticism or disbelief. I could feel the tension in the room, the impatience, the subtle judgment.

But I refused to let frustration cloud my resolve. Every response, every pause, every tone of my voice was a statement of integrity. I realized that defending myself wasn't just about this case; it was about standing for what was right in the midst of injustice. It was about showing the next generation that truth, courage, and composure mattered more than intimidation, assumption, or force.

The grand jury seemed endless. Hours stretched into days. I listened as attorneys debated, as witnesses spoke, as prosecutors attempted to weave a narrative I did not recognize. And yet, I learned to navigate this theater with calm observation, strategic answers, and mental clarity. My training in the streets, my experience on Rikers, and the discipline I had built into my life all converged in those moments.

One question from the foreman cut through the tension: "Have you ever been in a lineup or photo array?" My answer was simple: "No." It was a small answer, but it carried the weight of truth against presumption. The room seemed to pause; the foreman's inquiry was not just procedural — it was a test of character, and I held my ground.

Through this ordeal, I realized that the law is not always the same as justice. The grand jury was a reminder that systems are imperfect, that decisions are made in the shadow of bias and human error. But I also saw that the way one carries themselves in the face of systemic pressure can define the outcome as much as the law itself.

By the time the process concluded, I had learned invaluable lessons about resilience, strategic thinking, and the power of truth. I walked out with more than relief; I walked out with clarity. Every challenge, every questioning, every unjust assumption was a lesson in how to navigate authority, influence outcomes, and maintain integrity under pressure.

That experience became a foundation for my later work in leadership and advocacy. I understood that real change required not only courage but also a deep understanding of how systems operate, and how to use knowledge, observation, and strategy to protect those who cannot protect themselves.

Chapter 7, Part 4 — Mentorship & Community Leadership

Emerging from the challenges of Rikers and the grand jury, I realized that personal survival was not enough. The streets, the system, and the neighborhoods I had grown up in demanded more than resilience — they demanded action, guidance, and leadership. I couldn't just survive for myself; I needed to create pathways for others to thrive where too many had stumbled.

That realization sparked the foundation of mentorship as a central part of my life. I knew firsthand how much a single conversation, a guiding hand, or an example of discipline could change a young person's trajectory. It was not about telling them what to do, but showing them through experience, honesty, and presence.

I began small. I would walk through the neighborhoods, noticing youth loitering, frustrated, or misdirected. I would approach them, not with judgment, but with questions: "What are your goals? What do you want to see in your life? Who believes in you?" Often, these questions were the first time anyone had asked them directly.

I learned that mentorship required trust, and trust wasn't given lightly. Many kids had been let down by adults in the past.

They were wary, guarded, sometimes even hostile. So I had to prove my authenticity through consistency, patience, and presence. I attended basketball games, school events, and block parties, showing up when others would not. Every small interaction reinforced the principle that mentorship was built on credibility and reliability.

In these interactions, I discovered the transformative power of storytelling as a teaching tool. I shared my own experiences — the arrests, the jail time, the mistakes — not to glorify them, but to illustrate the consequences of choices and the value of learning from every experience. When a young person heard that someone who had been in the same neighborhoods, faced similar dangers, and survived was willing to invest time in them, they listened differently.

Leadership also meant creating structures to scale the impact. It wasn't enough to mentor a handful of youth; I wanted the programs to reach the next generation and the next, long after I was no longer physically present. I began developing formal programs, recruiting volunteers, and establishing protocols that ensured mentorship could operate effectively at every level.

Each mentor I trained became a multiplier. They carried the lessons forward, guiding other youth with the same principles of honesty, integrity, and accountability. I realized that true leadership was about leaving a legacy of empowerment — not just influence through presence, but through systems that could grow and thrive independently.

Through these efforts, I also learned about the delicate balance between guidance and autonomy. Young people needed direction, but they also needed to make their own decisions, succeed on their own terms, and fail safely when necessary. Part of mentorship was watching from the sidelines, ready to intervene when needed, but allowing room for growth, experimentation, and personal responsibility.

By the end of this phase of my work, mentorship had become more than a program — it was a philosophy, a way of life. It shaped not only the youth I guided but also the adults I worked with, creating a community of accountability, support, and shared vision. Each success reinforced the truth I had learned on the streets and in the courts: invest in people, and they will invest in the world around them.

Chapter 7, Part 5 — Building Systems That Last

It became clear that mentorship alone wasn't enough. Showing up, speaking to youth, or even organizing events could help temporarily, but if there were no structures to sustain the work, the impact would fade the moment I wasn't present. I needed to design systems that could operate independently, that could teach, guide, and uplift even without my daily supervision.

I started by mapping out every aspect of our programs. After-school activities, community workshops, youth mentoring sessions — each required clear protocols, training guides, and accountability mechanisms. I worked closely with volunteers, taking the time to teach not just the 'how' but the 'why'. Every activity had a purpose: to instill responsibility, resilience, and opportunity.

We developed tracking mechanisms to monitor progress. Attendance, engagement, skill development — each metric was carefully recorded and analyzed. If a program wasn't working, we adapted it. If a volunteer struggled, we provided additional support. I realized that systems were not static; they had to evolve with the needs of the community and the challenges of the moment.

Building these systems taught me the importance of sustainability. It was no longer about my personal energy or charisma — it was about creating frameworks that would endure beyond any single person. Volunteers were trained to become leaders in their own right, able to mentor, manage, and innovate independently. Youth participants could eventually become mentors themselves, passing on lessons to the next generation.

One of the most powerful lessons I learned in this process was about leverage. With a single, well-structured system, a small team could reach dozens, hundreds, or even thousands of young people. Impact multiplied exponentially. A program that seemed modest at first could, with the right design, influence entire neighborhoods.

In the process of building systems, I also confronted my own limitations. I realized I could not be everywhere, solve every problem, or personally mentor every child in need. The solution was architecture over presence — creating processes that did the work even when I wasn't physically there. This mindset reshaped how I approached leadership: from reactive to proactive, from temporary to permanent.

By the end of this phase, I saw the results. Programs ran smoothly, youth engagement improved, and the community began to internalize the lessons we were teaching. Volunteers and youth alike felt empowered because they were active participants in the design and execution. The systems were no longer just tools; they had become a living, evolving reflection of the values we believed in: integrity, loyalty, and empowerment.

Building systems was more than leadership; it was legacy creation. Each program, each protocol, each mentor trained was a seed planted for the future. The lessons learned here — patience, foresight, adaptability — became the blueprint for all my future advocacy work. It was proof that true leadership is measured not just in deeds but in the structures you leave behind that can continue to do good long after your own work is done.

Chapter 7, Part 6 — Advocacy and Outreach

Once the systems were in place, I realized that the work needed to extend beyond the walls of our programs. Mentorship and structured activities were powerful, but real change required engagement with the broader community, the city, and even local policymakers. Advocacy became the bridge between individual empowerment and systemic transformation.

I started attending community board meetings, city council forums, and public hearings. Every time I spoke, I drew from my own experiences — the streets, the hardships, the arrests, the lessons learned. My goal was clear: to ensure that the youth in our neighborhoods had voices, opportunities, and support systems that I had once lacked.

Outreach was not just about visibility; it was about creating partnerships. I reached out to local schools, religious institutions, and businesses, demonstrating how they could play a role in mentorship, provide resources, and offer safe spaces for youth. I emphasized the importance of collaboration over competition, showing that the community itself could be a network of support rather than a collection of isolated efforts.

One of the most important elements of advocacy was storytelling as truth-telling. I shared the realities of street life, the pitfalls that had ensnared so many, and the successes of those who had been guided toward better choices. These stories were powerful tools, not to glorify struggle but to illustrate consequences, resilience, and the possibility of transformation.

I also began creating programs specifically for parents and guardians, teaching them how to engage with their children, reinforce positive behaviors, and navigate systems that often seemed indifferent to their struggles. Many adults had experienced the streets themselves, and I had to meet them where they were — with empathy, patience, and practical guidance.

Media and technology became a part of our outreach strategy. Social media, community newsletters, and local radio allowed us to broadcast messages of hope, awareness, and opportunity. I made sure that the message was consistent: the community could take responsibility for its youth, empower them with resources, and change the trajectory of entire neighborhoods.

Advocacy also meant pushing for policy changes. I met with council members, spoke with nonprofit coalitions, and participated in panels about youth crime prevention, education equity, and safe recreational spaces. Every conversation was a chance to translate street knowledge into actionable policy, showing that solutions needed to be informed by those closest to the problem.

Through outreach and advocacy, I learned a profound truth: leadership is not about authority; it's about influence and responsibility. The more people I could inspire, teach, and mobilize, the more enduring our impact became. Each small victory — a child entering college, a parent reconnecting with their child, a community event that brought neighbors together — was proof that systemic change begins with committed, persistent action.

By the end of this phase, I understood that empowerment was multi-layered: it wasn't enough to guide individuals; the structures, policies, and culture of the community itself had to evolve. This work taught me that lasting change requires vision, strategy, and relentless execution — qualities that would carry me forward into the final stages of my leadership and into the legacy I hoped to leave.

Chapter 7, Part 7 — Forward Vision & Legacy

As the systems, programs, and advocacy efforts matured, I began to think beyond the immediate impact. Leadership, I realized, was not just measured by today's successes, but by the enduring structures and values left behind for future generations. Forward vision meant planning for decades, not months, and ensuring that the work would continue without me at the center.

I envisioned a community where mentorship was a standard, not an exception. Where youth had access to opportunities, guidance, and safe spaces — not because of luck or chance, but because the infrastructure of care, education, and empowerment was embedded into the neighborhood itself. Every program, every protocol, every volunteer trained was a building block toward that vision.

Legacy, I understood, was more than personal accolades or recognition. It was about shaping culture and expectation, showing young people that integrity, resilience, and responsibility could create pathways to success, even in the most challenging environments. I worked to ensure that the principles I valued — loyalty, honesty, diligence, and service — were woven into every part of our operations, from mentorship sessions to citywide initiatives.

I also reflected on the families in the community. Too often, parents were overlooked, struggling silently. I emphasized programs that engaged the entire household, teaching parents how to guide, protect, and support their children. The goal was holistic change: empowering youth while strengthening the foundations of the families who raised them.

Forward vision also meant preparing for scale. I considered how programs could expand across neighborhoods and boroughs, how partnerships could multiply our impact, and how lessons learned locally could influence citywide policy. Every strategy was built with sustainability in mind — a network of leaders, mentors, and community members capable of carrying the mission forward.

I thought about the next generation — my children, my grandchildren, and every child who walked through our programs. I imagined a world where they would not have to navigate the streets alone, where they would inherit not chaos, but guidance, opportunity, and a community invested in their success. That vision became the compass for every decision, every plan, and every new initiative.

By the time this chapter of my life was concluding, I realized that true leadership is timeless. It transcends individual action and becomes a living framework for others to follow. Legacy is not merely remembered — it is felt, lived, and perpetuated by those who inherit the structures, lessons, and principles laid down before them.

And so, as I looked ahead, I committed to ensure that my work, my lessons, and my values would continue to shape lives long after I was gone, creating a cycle of empowerment and hope that could endure for generations to come.

Chapter 8 — Answers and Solutions

Part 1: Personal Accountability

Accountability is one of the hardest lessons a person can truly internalize. It's easy to point fingers, blame circumstances, or rationalize mistakes, but life does not bend to excuses. The moment we take ownership of our actions, choices, and their consequences, we begin to unlock power — the kind that changes our trajectory, shapes relationships, and builds respect.

I learned accountability in the streets long before I saw it in classrooms or boardrooms. Every choice I made — good or bad — rippled outward, affecting friends, family, and the community. One wrong decision could lead to a night in jail; one right choice could save a life. Accountability is not reactive; it's proactive. It requires clarity about who you are, what you want, and how your actions affect those around you.

I teach the youth I mentor about the 3 C's of Accountability:

- Clarity: Understand your role in every situation. Know the difference between actions within your control and circumstances outside it. Recognize patterns in behavior that either lift you or weigh you down.

- Commitment: Once you acknowledge responsibility, commit to change. The promise to yourself is more important than anyone else's approval. Stay consistent. Show up every day, even when it's uncomfortable.

- Consequences: Accept the outcomes — rewards or penalties. Learning to sit with the result of your actions, without deflection or blame, is the core of growth. Consequences are lessons dressed in reality.

I tell the youth: if you cheat, lie, or fail to honor your word, the world will remember before you do. But if you stand by your word, even when nobody is watching, you create a foundation of trust that will carry you further than any street hustle, any degree, or any paycheck. A person breaking their word can lose more than money; it can cost friendships, opportunities, or even safety. Conversely, a person keeping their word can unlock doors that seem impossible to open.

Accountability is also about self-reflection. Daily, I look at my actions, the words I use, and the promises I make. I ask myself: Did I honor my values today? Did I act in a way that aligns with the man I want my children and grandchildren to emulate? If not, I adjust immediately. This habit became a cornerstone of my growth — in life, in leadership, and in community service.

Even at moments when I faced legal trouble or personal loss, holding myself accountable allowed me to survive, learn, and transform. It's a discipline that builds resilience and trustworthiness, qualities that are rarer than talent, more valuable than gold, and more enduring than fame.

Practical Tip: Write down your daily choices and reflect on how each action impacts others. Use it as a roadmap for improvement, no matter how small the steps may seem.

Hotline Resource: If you need guidance on accountability, life direction, or mental health support, call 1-800-662-4357 (SAMHSA). Professionals are there to guide you without judgment — a reminder that accountability starts with recognizing when help is necessary.

Chapter 8 — Answers and Solutions

Part 2: Community Strategies

No individual can thrive in isolation, and no neighborhood can transform without collective effort. Over the years, I've realized that creating meaningful change requires intentional strategies, not random acts of goodwill. Communities need structures, plans, and systems that allow residents to lift each other up, protect each other, and sustain progress over time.

Experts identify six strategies of community change:

7. Mass Mobilization – Rallying people toward a shared goal. It's the power of thousands acting with a single purpose, whether it's a neighborhood cleanup, a food drive, or a campaign to create safer streets. In the Bronx, we organized community events where hundreds of neighbors came together to reclaim public spaces and establish pride in the block. The energy from mass mobilization is contagious; it creates momentum that cannot be ignored.

8. Social Action – Taking deliberate steps to address injustices and inequities. This could mean organizing petitions, hosting educational forums, or confronting a problem head-on. Social action is about visibility and accountability, demonstrating that residents will not remain silent in the face of harm or neglect.

9. Citizen Participation – Everyone must have a voice. Encouraging residents to join community boards, attend city council meetings, or volunteer in youth programs ensures that decisions reflect lived experience. It is remarkable how often the people closest to a problem have the best solutions; the trick is getting them to speak up and act.

10. Public Advocacy – Engaging with policymakers, agencies, and local leaders to influence decisions. Over my years with I Am My Community Inc, I've learned that a single letter, phone call, or personal visit can create ripples that change entire systems. Advocacy is not confrontation; it's presenting facts, lived experience, and actionable solutions in a way that leaders cannot ignore.

11. Popular Education – Knowledge is power. Sharing what you know empowers others to take action. We created workshops, mentorship programs, and community seminars that teach youth about safety, opportunity, and leadership. Educated residents become agents of change, passing on skills, awareness, and insight to the next generation.

12. Local Services Development – Building programs that address real needs: food pantries, after-school activities, mental health workshops, and skill-building courses. These services create tangible impact while teaching accountability, responsibility, and community values.

I have seen firsthand how these strategies intersect. A youth mentorship program might involve education, citizen participation, and local services simultaneously. When residents feel empowered to take ownership of their neighborhood, change becomes self-sustaining.

Actionable Advice: If you want to change your community, start small. Attend a local meeting, organize a block cleanup, or mentor a child. Momentum grows from consistent effort, and your actions will inspire others to join.

Hotline/Resource: For guidance on community organizing or volunteer opportunities, call 1-866-827-3747 (NeighborWorks America). They provide support and structure for residents looking to build safer, stronger communities.

Chapter 8 — Answers and Solutions

Part 3: Education & Opportunity

Education is the foundation of possibility. I have always believed that knowledge is power, and access to education is a lifeline for communities like mine. The streets teach lessons about survival, loyalty, and resourcefulness, but formal education equips a person to navigate systems, claim opportunity, and break cycles of hardship.

From a young age, I saw the value of learning. While my peers were hustling or getting lost in distractions, I found ways to expand my mind and sharpen my skills. In my nonprofit work with I Am My Community Inc, I emphasize to youth and parents that the resources exist — often free — if we choose to take advantage of them. GED classes, OSHA 40-hour courses, and CDL licenses are not just credentials; they are tools that open doors, shift mindsets, and give young people options beyond the block.

I tell youth: "Education can be the coolest thing on the block." It starts with framing it as a choice, a challenge, and a personal victory. When a young person passes a GED test or earns a certification, it is celebrated like a championship. This recognition builds confidence, fosters pride, and reinforces the message that success is possible.

Summer youth jobs are another powerful avenue. By engaging in structured work, kids earn money, build experience, and see a world outside the immediate pressures of their neighborhood. I've watched young people transform after just one summer of mentorship, work, and exposure to professional standards. It's proof that opportunity changes behavior and perspective.

Parents play a vital role. Signing kids up for programs, encouraging them to attend classes, celebrating small wins — these are not optional actions; they are investments in a lifetime of impact. Showing interest and participating in their growth communicates a message stronger than any lecture.

Practical Tip: Take inventory of the resources around you. Many community colleges, technical schools, and online programs offer free or low-cost courses. Sign up, encourage others, and make learning visible and celebrated.

Hotline/Resource: For GED programs and educational guidance, call 1-800-628-0222 (GED Testing Service). For additional career and skill-building programs, check local community centers or colleges.

Education and opportunity are not abstract ideals; they are actionable pathways. The youth of today can leverage these tools to break cycles, elevate families, and reshape neighborhoods. With mentorship, access, and encouragement, knowledge becomes the most powerful currency a young person can earn.

Chapter 8 — Answers and Solutions

Part 4: Advocacy & Policy Change

Change does not happen in isolation. To transform a community, to protect its youth, and to ensure opportunity, we must understand the structures that govern us and actively participate in shaping them. Advocacy and policy change are not just for elected officials; they are tools every resident can wield to make neighborhoods safer, stronger, and more equitable.

I learned early that many people don't know who represents them, which community board governs their building, or even the district they live in. This knowledge is power, and with it comes the responsibility to act. It begins with asking questions, attending local meetings, and making your voice heard.

Advocacy can take many forms:

- Writing letters or emails to your local representatives.

- Attending community board sessions to present issues affecting your block.

- Organizing neighborhood meetings to discuss challenges and solutions.

- Collaborating with nonprofits to lobby for programs, funding, or legislation.

Real advocacy is persistent and informed. It requires research, patience, and the ability to present lived experience as credible evidence. I've walked into meetings and heard skepticism, yet every story, every fact shared, was a testament to the power of being prepared and committed. Change is not instantaneous, but when community members engage collectively, even small actions accumulate into systemic progress.

Policy change is intertwined with awareness. Residents must push for transparency, accountability, and the protection of youth. For example, advocating for after-school programs, safer parks, or youth employment opportunities directly impacts lives. Policies aren't abstract rules; they are instruments that shape everyday experiences. A policy that funds summer youth jobs or GED programs may be the difference between a teen walking toward opportunity or being pulled into crime.

Practical Tip: Identify your elected officials — city council, state assembly, or local boards — and commit to engaging with at least one issue this year. Volunteer, attend hearings, or provide testimony. Every voice counts, and your lived experience matters.

Hotline/Resource: For guidance on civic engagement or local advocacy programs, visit www.nyc.gov or call 311 for local government services.

True leadership is about empowering others to understand and influence the systems around them. Advocacy and policy change are not optional; they are essential for building sustainable, thriving communities. By teaching youth and adults to engage, we create a culture where solutions are pursued collectively, and the next generation grows up knowing that their voice matters.

Chapter 8 — Answers and Solutions

Part 5: Family & Parenting Solutions

Being a parent is one of the most challenging and rewarding roles a person can hold. It is not about being friends; it is about guiding, protecting, and preparing the next generation for life's realities. I've learned that the smallest gestures — saying "I love you," showing up consistently, setting clear boundaries — can shape a child's world far more than grandiose promises ever could.

From the day my first daughter was born, I understood the weight of responsibility. At 17, I was still a child myself, yet I had to step into a role that demanded maturity, discipline, and foresight. Every decision mattered. Every action had ripple effects. I taught my children that respect is reciprocal, that boundaries are necessary, and that love must be demonstrated daily.

Time and communication are at the core of effective parenting. It's not enough to be present physically; parents must engage emotionally and mentally. I structured my days to attend school events, participate in trips, and make myself available to answer questions, solve problems, and instill values. I wanted my children to know that while mistakes happen, there is always a safe space to learn and grow.

Discipline is a cornerstone, but it is more than punishment. It is teaching accountability, helping children understand consequences for choices, and ensuring that the lessons last beyond the moment. By modeling responsible behavior, showing honesty, and maintaining integrity, parents can empower children to navigate life independently.

I also emphasize the importance of professional help when needed. Mental health, counseling, and guidance are not signs of weakness; they are tools for resilience. Families that communicate openly and normalize seeking help foster emotional intelligence, stability, and long-term success.

Practical Advice:

- Establish daily rituals of connection, even brief check-ins.

- Set clear rules and expectations that are consistent.

- Celebrate achievements — big and small — to reinforce growth.

- Demonstrate love openly; children internalize actions, not just words.

Hotline/Resource: For parenting support or family guidance, call 1-800-422-4453 (National Parent Helpline).

Parenting is the foundation of community transformation. By shaping responsible, resilient, and empowered children, we invest in the future of neighborhoods, cities, and generations. Every lesson, every conversation, every moment matters. Family solutions are not temporary fixes; they are the blueprint for generational success.

Chapter 8 — Answers and Solutions

Part 6: Maintaining Hope, Mental Health & Forward Vision

Hope is not passive; it is an active choice, a daily decision to keep moving forward even when circumstances feel insurmountable. I have seen the devastation that lack of guidance, untreated trauma, and unchecked mental health challenges can create in neighborhoods like mine. Too often, communities normalize suffering — the gunfire, the losses, the instability — and fail to recognize that healing is a responsibility we all share.

Mental health is as critical as any other aspect of survival. Many individuals in the Bronx and similar communities carry trauma they barely understand. They adapt by numbing emotions or embracing the chaos around them, but untreated mental illness can lead to despair, risky behaviors, and generational patterns of pain. Recognizing and addressing mental health is an act of courage.

I encourage youth, parents, and community members to view mental health as a resource, not a stigma. Therapy, counseling, and guidance are not privileges; they are lifelines. I've made sure that through I Am My Community Inc, resources and access to professionals are available — because a single conversation or intervention can redirect a life.

Hotline/Resources:

- National Alliance on Mental Illness (NAMI): 1-800-950-6264

- SAMHSA Helpline: 1-800-662-4357

Forward vision means planning for sustainability, impact, and legacy. I've built I Am My Community Inc with systems that continue beyond my direct involvement — mentorship programs, youth initiatives, community workshops — ensuring that lessons, opportunities, and guidance persist across generations. Leadership is not measured by the present alone; it is judged by the structures left for those who come next.

Maintaining hope requires action. I encourage everyone to invest in themselves, seek help when needed, and commit to being a stabilizing force for others. Every effort to educate, mentor, or guide a youth, every initiative to improve a neighborhood, is a direct investment in hope.

Finally, the collective legacy is a culmination of our work, values, and vision. I envision a Bronx and neighborhoods like it where children grow up with opportunity, adults collaborate instead of compete destructively, and communities thrive because people choose accountability, care, and action every day. This vision is alive in every program we run, every life we touch, and every lesson we impart.

Resource & Website: For ongoing community engagement and programs, visit www.iammycommunityinc.com.

Epilogue — Family, Grandchildren, and Legacy

As I sit back and reflect on the life I've lived, I see the threads that connect everything: the streets, the struggles, the victories, the losses, and the lessons. And at the center of it all, standing as the most profound source of joy and purpose, are my grandchildren. Six lives, three boys and three girls, ranging from just two months old to twenty years, each carrying their own energy, curiosity, and promise.

My grandchildren are a mirror of hope. Every time I walk into a room where they are laughing, playing, or asking questions, I see the future I fought for, the lives I hoped to influence, and the cycles I wanted to break. There is no pretense with them — in their eyes, I am not defined by my mistakes, my arrests, or my time in the system. I am grandad, grandp, granddaddy — a constant in their world, someone who shows up, listens, and loves without condition.

During summer breaks, I take them under my wing for the entire season. We fill the days with exploration, adventure, and learning: trips to museums, community events, parks, and local neighborhoods that I know shaped me. We laugh together, and sometimes we get quiet, sharing stories that reveal the complexity of life, the importance of choices, and the resilience of the human spirit. Nights are filled with movies, whispered advice, and conversations that linger long after the lights go out.

Distance has never diminished these bonds. Though my grandchildren live in North Carolina and I reside in the Bronx, our connection is constant. Phone calls, video chats, and letters keep our conversations alive. When they return to visit, it's as if no time has passed at all — their energy fills the house, and I am reminded that legacy is not measured in proximity, but in the love, guidance, and attention we pour into those we cherish.

Watching my grandchildren grow has also reaffirmed a truth I have carried for decades: the importance of building systems that endure beyond our presence. The lessons I teach them, the principles I instill, the values I model — these are all part of a living legacy that they will carry forward, influencing their peers, their communities, and eventually their own children.

My dreams for the family extend beyond moments of laughter and joy. I envision a home large enough to house every child and grandchild, a place where we can gather, celebrate, and continue the cycle of mentorship and guidance. I want every one of them to feel the safety, love, and opportunities I strived to create, so that they can thrive without the obstacles that challenged me.

But legacy is not only about family. It is also about community, service, and the choices we make in shaping the world around us. Every program I built, every youth I mentored, every advocate I trained — these are extensions of the same philosophy that drives me with my grandchildren: invest in people, nurture potential, and leave the world better than you found it.

As I look forward, I see that life is a continuum. The lessons of the past, the work of the present, and the vision for the future are all intertwined. My grandchildren are a daily reminder that what we build today can inspire, protect, and empower generations yet to come. In their eyes, I see hope. In their laughter, I hear purpose. And in their dreams, I recognize the reflection of everything I fought to create — a legacy of resilience, love, and unwavering commitment to people, family, and community.

The story does not end here. It lives on in each child mentored, every program sustained, and every grandchild nurtured. The life I have led, the choices I have made, and the systems I have built — all converge to form a simple truth: we are the stewards of the future, and it is our responsibility to leave it better than we found it.

About the Author

Darney K. "K Born" Rivers is a Bronx native whose life story embodies resilience, transformation, and dedication to community. From humble beginnings in the Bronx, he navigated the challenges of urban life, early loss, and legal struggles to emerge as a leader, mentor, and advocate for youth and families.

As the founder of I Am My Community Inc, Darney has created sustainable programs that empower young people, provide resources for families, and cultivate safer, stronger neighborhoods. His work spans mentorship, advocacy, education, and community engagement, reflecting a philosophy that the closest people to a problem often hold the keys to its solution.

Darney is also a celebrated artist, whose hip-hop legacy spans decades. He is known for his landmark track "New Generation", produced by Teddy Riley, which helped define a new era in music. Beyond music, Darney's life experiences — from navigating the streets, incarceration, and personal loss — inform his writing, teaching, and public service.

He has been recognized with numerous awards, proclamations, and community honors, and he continues to work tirelessly to build systems of empowerment, leaving a legacy for future generations.

Through his memoir, Darney shares hard-earned lessons on accountability, leadership, survival, and hope, offering readers a blueprint to navigate life's challenges and create meaningful change in their own communities.

Author's Note

This memoir is not about perfection. It is about evolution, about the mistakes that teach, the hardships that shape, and the redemption that follows. It is about loyalty, resilience, and the courage it takes to stand up even when the world seems determined to keep you down.

I did not write these pages to glorify the past, nor to present myself as someone without flaws. I wrote this book because stories have the power to save lives. To inspire someone, to guide someone, to help someone see that even in the darkest corners, there is a path forward.

Within these chapters, you will find the streets I grew up on, the lessons learned from family, mentors, and mistakes, and the work I have done to transform pain into purpose. You will meet the people who shaped me, the challenges that tested me, and the victories that reminded me of the power of perseverance.

If even one young person reads these pages and chooses a better path, if even one family finds guidance in these stories, then every moment spent writing, reflecting, and remembering has been worth it.